Updated For 2009-

The New

Survival Guide

To

Foreclosure

All the information you need to know to survive a foreclosure and restore your credit

D1430513

Written By

Clyde R. Goulet

ISBN: 1-4392-0585-X
ISBN-13: 9781439205853

Visit www.booksurge.com to order additional copies.

Table of Contents

2009 Revisions & Updates

When I put this book together back in 2005 I had no way of knowing how the housing market would crumble like it has in many areas of the country.

I did predict to anyone who would listen that based on the loans that were being written that there would be another huge wave of Foreclosures. Believe me, I am not that smart but I do know what a risky loan looks like. The flood of 80% first mortgages combined with 20% second mortgages in my mind was a recipe for disaster. A person with shaky credit getting into adjustable rate mortgages and having none of their own money at stake was just plain stupid. That goes for both the lender and the consumer.

Then there are the people who took advantage of the double digit appreciation rates and pulled huge chunks of inflated "equity" out of their properties. Certainly some took advantage of the feeding frenzy and had every intention of paying the money back. Other used it as an opportunity to pick up a chunk of cash with no designs of paying a dime of it back.

There is enough blame to go around here that is for sure. From the lenders bending over backwards to get anyone with a pulse qualified for a loan to the general public that was lured in with the promises of easy credit and home ownership. Can you blame the consumer for jumping at a chance for home ownership especially since owning a home is still very much a part of the American Dream?

That dream has turned into a nightmare of epic if not historic proportions in many parts of the country. Since many of the loans that were originated before the collapse at the end of 2006 have yet to have their first adjustment, I will predict again that this foreclosure mess will continue for at least a couple of years until all those risky loans get shaken out of the system.

The Government in their infinite stupidity has begun pointing fingers and now are taking down some of the players in the Wall Street circle that they perceive to be the culprits. While Congress wrings their hands over how to make this a political issue, the people in need of the most help remain the victims in many ways.

Perhaps if the individual tax burden was not so huge for our bloated federal government, maybe allowing people to keep more of what they earn in their pockets might be the best and quickest remedy for a weak economy and sluggish housing market. Never mind, that makes way too much sense, it will never happen. In the meantime we must all do our best to protect our wallets, self interest, and our families in any way possible.

This book was revamped to account for some of the changes that have occurred on the lender side of things as well as the consumer side of the equation. I will detail some of the case histories I have worked on that will both surprise you and maybe give you some reason for hope.

The lenders are literally choking at the volume of these foreclosure cases. What used to take a couple of months to complete has pushed into the five or six month time period. That is a positive for the property owner as it gives them more time to either work out a solution with their lenders or gives them more time to get back on their feet and move on.

While this mess continues there are very few people qualified to assist property owners through this mess. I have tried unsuccessfully to get the local Real Estate board to allow me to teach to Realtors how to assist property owners through the Foreclosure process and teach them how to work Short Sales for the people who needed to sell their homes in order to just move on and save their credit from a full blown Foreclosure. It has fallen on deaf ears.

I have personally decided to try and get financial professionals involved. I am reaching out to people such as your Accountant or CPA that may handle your tax returns that are familiar with you and your finances. Basically someone you can trust to give you straight answers and will not be intimidated by the Short Sale process. It makes total sense to get these types of professionals involved and I do believe that all parties will be served best.

Without further delay or comments about our inept Governments attempt to come up with a solution, I will prod forward and update this book to make it as fresh as possible amidst the changes in the real estate market that seem to occur on an almost daily basis. Unfortunately, there is not a quick fix for this national problem, but like all other down real estate cycles I have seen in my life, this too shall pass and the market will rebound once again.

My hope and prayers are with the families that may be torn apart by the financial burdens and stress these foreclosures and potential bankruptcies cause. In an election year we are sure to see this topic surface in some way, shape or form. I also want to offer anyone picking up this book some additional resources to combat your tough economic times.

I have put together a FREE e-mail course on how to protect yourselves further from your financial difficulties. Simply log on to www.clydegoulet.com and look for the FREE e-course on the menu options. You will be directed to a sign up page and will be asked to confirm your e-mail address via a double opt in permission process. I hate junk e-mail and I just want to make sure that we have your o.k. to send the FREE e-course.

I look forward to sending you this new updated, free information as time goes on we hope that your situation changes and that you are back on your financial feet quickly. I wish you all the best, take care and God bless.

Chapter 1

Foreclosure – It Happened to Me Too!

The prospect of an impending foreclosure can leave many homeowners feeling overwhelmed and confused to the point of feeling totally powerless to control their fate. It was by far one of the most stressful experiences of my life and it also put a heavy strain on my marriage. I thank God my wife stood by me when things were at their worst. It certainly helps us appreciate the blessings that we now share and took for granted in the past.

There wasn't anything in my past experiences that could have prepared me for the four to six months leading up to our filing our Chapter 13 bankruptcy. The threatening calls, the feeling of defeat, and the outright ignorance I had for what was happening to us and the poor advice and misinformation we received from supposedly professional people was just devastating.

The first hand experiences and what I have learned since my own foreclosure and bankruptcy has compelled me to share what I have learned and pass this information along to as many people as possible. Will it help everyone? I doubt it, but if it helps just one family stay together, or helps to save their home, then it is well worth the time, research, and energy it has taken to put this book together.

I continue today to offer free, no obligation foreclosure counseling to people in pre-foreclosure or approaching foreclosure as to what to expect and what options they still have remaining. As you will see later in this book, the banks and mortgage companies who are initiating the foreclosures do not always tell you the whole story or give you the complete picture.

We are also helping homeowners in foreclosure by actively negotiating with banks and mortgage companies to reduce debt owed on behalf of homeowners. The negotiating work we do with first and second mortgages assist homeowners and help to keep many properties out of foreclosure. We will discuss in detail the process called a "short sale" or "short payoff" and how it can help get you out from under your mountain of debt. I will take you step by step through this process and detail what properties are better candidates than others. You will find out the real reason why banks do not want to own your property or anyone else's, for that matter.

If you have multiple mortgages and liens on your property, I will explain in detail some of the very best strategies for negotiating them down to literally pennies on the dollar and in some cases completely written off by the debtor. You will discover why a second mortgage holder becomes very eager to get something, sometimes anything for their second mortgages.

There is a beginning, middle, and end to the foreclosure process that every person going through the process should be aware of. I have been through that process myself and can help you to understand exactly what to expect and what to do once the dust has settled in order to get back on your financial feet.

This book is simply a comprehensive guide to the foreclosure process, an outline detailing how to save your home, and a guide to help plan your financial recovery. It is also a "hands on" guide on how to sell your house and get back into the ranks of the homeowners of the world in a very short period of time.

As financially bleak as it sometimes was, we were able to re-build our credit to the point of assisting us in an active real estate investment company today. It would have taken much less time to re-build that credit if I had known what I know today and will pass along to you later in this book. There is a complete sub-industry out there specializing in credit restoration, you just have to know where to look.

⚜ MY REAL LIFE STORY ⚜

As I spill out my true, no-holds-barred story of what led to our financial troubles, I realize there are other, more tragic stories out there with far more pain and suffering. We were truly blessed to have what happened to us happen at the time it did. The circumstances brought us back closer to the church and my faith and taught us what was really important in life. This book is also a manifestation of those events.

Foreclosure – It Happened to Me Too!

The story begins with an all too familiar scene where we were quite honestly living just beyond our means. We had moved down to central Florida from the Northeast in 1990 and I was fortunate to find a job in the field of my studies, accounting.

I quickly learned that the pay scales in Florida were not in step with the pay scales of the Northeast. I took a job as the assistant controller for a commercial real estate company in Orlando Florida that did property management as well, another area where I had extensive experience.

My wife was unable to work due to a bi-polar condition that was for the most part under control with medication of various doses and combinations. She maintained a relatively normal life considering Mary is also deaf. At the time her medications were working sometimes; and other times not working very well at all. Basically, she was in and out of depression and up and down like a yo-yo.

The trouble began when her regular doctor took an extended one-month vacation out of the country and left a doctor in charge with much less experience and what would later turn out to be, extremely poor judgment. After calling this replacement doctor for an unscheduled visit, the doctor was convinced that my wife was faking her condition and drastically cut her medication, with devastating results.

The next few months, we did nothing but go back and forth to the doctors, back and forth to the hospital; and the ups and downs came with greater swings and with greater frequency. I had to make a choice, either go with my wife for all these appointments or not go since Mary was not able to drive herself. This took me away from my job and wore very thin very fast where I was working.

After about two months of this, my employer had pretty much told me they could no longer afford to pay me for not being there. Who could blame them, I was never there, and when I was I was worrying about my wife.

Once I was terminated, our credit was still very good and we were getting every credit card offer under the sun and I was applying for and getting credit lines with no problem. At one point, we had about twelve to fifteen credit cards and we were basically living off of them. This went on for a couple of months until the credit lines were maxed out and we could not borrow from one to pay the minimums anymore.

We began to fall behind on the mortgage payment of our primary residence as well as an investment property that was our former residence and eventually the process server delivered the foreclosure notices on both properties. By then we were four months behind on our primary residence and the tenant we had in the rental property had stopped paying and we were actually just about to start getting out of our financial hole when we got the notices. My wife was finally back working with her regular doctor, she was on a new medication that gave Mary her life back and I was working on my own as a commercial real estate broker.

The calls from the collections departments of the credit card companies and mortgage companies were endless. Not only were they persistent, they were downright rude. They accused me of everything except shooting Kennedy and if they couldn't get any money from us, they wanted our blood. I understand they were just doing their job, but I swear you must have to pass some sort of SOB test to qualify to work that type of job.

Maybe it was the guilt of wanting to do the right thing, or maybe I fell for a sales pitch, but we were convinced that filing a Chapter 13 bankruptcy would be the best thing to do. We were told it was the "only" way to save our primary residence. We went through and began the process and when the time came to sign off on our repayment plan, which is what the Chapter 13 is designed to do, pay back your creditors over time. Our repayment plan was for five years.

When we sat down with our bankruptcy attorney to sign off on our repayment plan, we were told our new monthly payment to the trustee would amount to $1,416.00 per month. Granted, we could not make the $863.00 mortgage payment on our house just a few months ago, I was convinced this attorney was on his own kind of drugs. I thought there was no way we would make this happen.

As I mentioned, we were on the road back to a recovery, or at least our monthly income was rebounding. My wife was even feeling good enough to take on a small part time job. The commercial real estate brokerage was starting to get off the ground, but like many real estate businesses that depend on commission income, the actual paydays were both unpredictable and were being spilt with a partner.

I even went and worked a couple of nights a week trading my hours for dollars just to get a few extra dollars coming in. Despite all this, we still needed the bank to work with us to restructure our payments. Since we had committed to the bankruptcy repayment plan, there was nothing the workout/loss mitigation department could do, their hands were tied.

To make a long story even longer, we wound up losing our investment property and despite our best efforts to do the right thing and pay all our creditors back, our credit was pretty much trash. It stayed that was for about five years after our case had been dismissed and even today in the summer of 2008 it will occasionally show up and we will have to produce documentation of the bankruptcy being discharged.

In hindsight, we probably should have simply filed for chapter 7 liquidation and start over fresh sooner. I have no real opinion on what would be best if you were to file for bankruptcy to save your home or not, but if it ever happens again, I will ask and get more answers to the questions I would certainly have for the attorney.

Later on in this book, I will rank by degree of negativity what every action we took had on our credit. In other words, you will see if simply having a note on your credit report that you signed a "deed in lieu of foreclosure" is more detrimental than having a full-blown foreclosure or bankruptcy.

✖ WHAT TO LOOK FORWARD TO ✖

In the chapters to follow we will cover a variety of topics that will assist you in understanding not only the process you will be going through, but understand that you are not alone and that you do indeed have more options than you think.

Chapter two will cover how to keep the balls in the air while you try and get back on your feet, if your financial problems are just a temporary bump in the road. We will explain sources of short-term funds and the resources you may be unaware of that are out there for people facing foreclosure.

In the third chapter of this book you will get a brief explanation of the loan and lien hierarchy and who carries the biggest stick. You may not be at all surprised as to what kind of liens and judgments do not go away with foreclosures. If nothing else, you will learn that sometimes the creditors making the most noise have very little power to do anything about their situation but will make darn sure they make your life miserable.

Chapter four will detail the best ways to handle the collections people and some strategies for not letting them stress you out too much. I will also go over some laws that pertain to collection calls that many people don't know about but could cause your creditor some serious problems if they break the rules.

Chapter five will begin the detailed discussion of strategies for saving your home and potentially helping put your financial life back together. We will get into great detail as to the documentation that will be needed to prove financial hardship to the bank and the main reasons why banks must work with you to create a repayment solution if the numbers work. The topic of restructuring debt and negotiating forbearance agreements with the people in loss mitigation will be discussed. At the end of this chapter, you will know what to ask these people and what to do if you get a person working your file in the loss mitigation department who will not work with you.

To follow in chapter six is the topic of whether to try and sell or keep the home would be an option to consider. You will hear my thoughts on overcoming the emotional attachment to a home or property that holds sentimental value. There will also be a lengthy discussion of the wolfs in sheep's clothing masquerading as investors trying to "help" you, when all they are trying to help is themselves to your equity if your home still has some.

Chapter seven will cover some of my personal experiences on how to position and sell your home at lightning speed if that is what you choose to do.

There are tips and strategies that most Realtors never even think about that will get potential buyers pounding on your door wanting to see your property.

Chapter eight will cover some of my personal experiences with our bankruptcy and my thoughts on what I certainly would have done differently had I known the long term consequences of our decisions. I will explain in non-legal terms the basic differences between Chapter 7 & Chapter 13 personal bankruptcy and what is expected from you the borrower.

Chapter nine will detail the steps needed to get you pointed in the right direction to getting your credit restored. Not only will I give you some practical advice on how to get this done, I will also share a couple of my real estate purchasing techniques that do not require you to go to a bank and qualify for a loan and gives you control of the property. You will be surprised how easy it can be to get back into a home of your own. This should be exciting news!

In chapter ten you will get a step by step tutorial on how to buy a house with no or bad credit and virtually no cash. You will see how I buy and control properties as an investor and convert that knowledge to some basic guidelines to follow when looking to get into that next house. This chapter alone is worth the cost of this book 100 times. Yes, you can buy real estate with no money down.

In chapter 11 I will get back on my soapbox of sorts and explain how my wife and I got back on our feet and our belief of what got us there quickly. The basic theme is simply that to get more out of life, you must give more. It is an amazing fact of life, but this chapter cannot be ignored and this law of nature cannot be broken.

The information contained in Chapter 12 is written for one reason; to help you protect yourself at all times. It is vitally important that you know exactly what you are getting into when you are signing documents or turning over control of your property in one way or another. This chapter was added from the original version of this book along with some updated information that has changed from the original publication.

✿ DON'T TAKE IT PERSONALLY ✿

I usually save my soapbox speech to the end of my discussions and in this case the end of the book. However, this topic is far too important to leave to the end since some of you may only read the first chapter and hopefully what you are about to read will have a positive impact on your preconceived thoughts about foreclosure and financial problems.

One of my favorite sayings is that, "I came into this world naked and broke; at least I will be leaving with a three piece suit." Since we all did come into this world naked, whatever we leave with is a bonus in my mind. In reality we all seem to worry about the "things" in our lives. The cars, the big screen TV's, the toys, and yes even the houses we live in.

Sure, we all need a roof over our heads and shelter and warmth is very important. However the special memories you have from your home will stay with you forever. I have great memories of growing up in the family home back in Massachusetts, but I knew I was never going to live my entire life there and die there as well. The house may be gone, but the memories will last forever. All I am saying is do not get too emotionally attached to your property. If you can find a way to save it, great you are ahead of the game. If it is lost through the foreclosure, pick up, move on and start again and don't look back except to learn from your mistakes.

If everyone only knew the amount of people going through the same or similar thing, you would not feel so alone. The current foreclosure mess is sweeping the country as a result of the sub-prime loans; entire neighborhoods are beginning to sit abandoned. Some of the most successful people in the world have suffered some devastating financial setbacks and defeats before they dusted themselves off and got back up. Ray Kroc of McDonalds' fame nearly went bankrupt many times when McDonalds was first starting out. In fact he did not take a salary for the first two to three years of his business.

It would have been very easy for me to blame all our financial problems on my wife and at times I did dump on Mary a bit, but the bottom line is that it was really no ones fault, it was just a dark part of our lives. I am the one who made the decision to be with my wife and if I had to do it over again, I would take the same path, no question about it.

Foreclosure – It Happened to Me Too!

I knew I still loved my wife very much, wanted her to have everything she wanted as long as we could afford it, and knew that we would bounce back. Please avoid the blame game and build on the positive things that are still part of your life. If you have children, think about them and their best interest. Is it healthier for them to be living in an environment where there is constant financial stress or would it be better for all if they were in a place where the issues are not related to the finances?

Focusing on the negative is human nature and just easier to do than counting your blessings and looking for the positive things in our lives. There is not a day that goes by in my life today that I do not take the time out of my day and give thanks for the blessings in my life. I also think that if someone had suggested I do that when we were having our financial problems, I would have told them to go take a hike.

Just look around, do you have a solid family and friends? Is your health O.K.? Do you have a marketable skill where you can earn a decent living? Are you living in the country where people are flocking to because they envy the freedom and opportunities we have here? You are richer than you think.

As we move onward in this book, I urge you to use it as intended, a simple reference guide to get you through this tough time and on to bigger, better things and maybe even into another house. Keep a pen and paper or highlighter ready; the information will come fast and furious. I know you will be wiser when you are finished this book, I hope it helps in some small way.

I am praying for you!

Chapter 2

Keeping All The Balls in The Air

There is no doubt that when we were headed to our foreclosure and bankruptcy, I did everything I could think of to postpone the inevitable. There is also little doubt that I had a serious case of denial going on that I did not want to admit, me with an accounting/business administration degree from a business school in the northeast, with three plus years of public accounting experience, had screwed up the finances so bad we were about to go under.

I was in the process of building a house of cards and the next stiff breeze was about to blow it all away. My particular house of cards was the mountain of credit card debt I was amassing just to survive until we were back on our feet. When you are paying 15% to 21% interest rates, you tend to not catch up in a hurry.

This chapter will deal with the many causes of foreclosure and some of the short-term fixes you might want to consider. I do not recommend many of these strategies; however in some cases I have found that the homeowner was clearly going to get back on their feet very quickly and utilizing credit lines or credit cards made perfect sense.

Before we get into some of the major reasons people get into such a mess in the first place, there are two topics that must be addressed. The first is: you are not alone. Seems like a pretty obvious statement at this time. Every day in the news or on line I read stories about the foreclosure rate being the highest in many years if not history.

The fact is they are correct in this particular case and that there are more foreclosures taking place now then ever before in the nations history. The second is: when credit was so easy to obtain in the lending environment of a few years ago, is it any wonder homeowners got into trouble when they are being bombarded with offers for refinancing their homes up to 125% of their current home values.

When we further take into account the double digit appreciation rate in some areas of the country with these risky loan offers and the result is the foreclosure avalanche. Combined with creative financing encouraged by some of the national builders where borrowers were approved for 80% first mortgages with a 20% second mortgage right behind. This created two problems:

The first was that many people getting into these newer developments were paying top dollar for the properties and they were, on paper, appreciating every month and everyone was happy. The lenders figured that the appreciation would continue to insure their position and those market prices would be sustained. Well, that did not happen. As a matter of fact market values began to decline and people could not sell their overpriced houses for anything near what they owed on them.

The second challenge evolved from the first. Since these new homeowners had very little and in some cases none of their own money at stake in the property, they began to bail out of the houses even before the property was officially foreclosed on. This has a ripple effect of creating a downward push on property values all around the subject property. The property is vacant, the grass grows to knee cap height and the neighborhood starts to look like a ghost town. Not a pretty sight and even less desirable if you are one of the property owners in that neighborhood who needs to sell and you are competing with vacant, bank owned properties. It is a vicious and unfortunate cycle.

❧ IT HAPPENS TO MORE PEOPLE THAN YOU KNOW. ❧

Foreclosures are at an all time high in our country. Is it that the economy is in tough shape? I doubt it; the economy is bad only if you allow it to be bad in your life. Certainly there are layoffs and downsizing in corporate America that can't be minimized, but jobs are plentiful and I will never use that as an excuse.

There are other factors that never change, such as sickness, death, and divorce. At the time of the update of this book, Orange County Florida, near and around Orlando had over 1,000 foreclosures filed in the first two months of 2008. Our economy is relatively steady here at the present time; properties are still relatively affordable, although values are declining in some areas. Interest rates were being juggled almost monthly by the FED and God only knows what the current rates are today. People were able to afford bigger houses with lower monthly payments before, now I'm not too sure.

Why would this rate of foreclosure be so high in an area that is booming with new businesses and adequate housing? I have found through my experience that when credit gets easy to obtain, people will usually overextend themselves. As mentioned above, the onslaught of home equity lines of credit offers I still get is just overwhelming. We are a society of instant gratification and credit cards and home equity lines of credit are just too damn convenient and easy to get. If the bank didn't make it so easy, would we take advantage of it?

You should also know that the price ranges of the houses in foreclosure in Orange County Florida referenced above range from small one bedroom one bath condo's valued at $75,000 to a mansion in the same subdivision where some famous professional athletes have multi million dollar homes. Foreclosure happens to the rich, poor, and everyone in between. Male, female, white, Hispanic, African- American, Jewish, Catholics, basically anyone and everyone could be a potential foreclosure candidate.

WHY BANKS AND MORTGAGE COMPANIES BEAR SOME BLAME

In my opinion, the banks and mortgage companies who relentlessly send us mounds of solicitations every blessed week to refinance our homes at a lower rate or take advantage of the equity that has built up in our homes, bear some of the responsibility for the foreclosure problems. Please don't get me wrong, the homeowner signing on the dotted line is ultimately responsible, it just makes no sense some of the financing products that are offered in this time in history.

They have made it far too easy for the consumer to get extra money for frivolous things we neither need nor can afford. As I have mentioned already, how stupid is it for a bank or mortgage company to let you borrow up to 125% of your homes value? They are asking for trouble if you ask me. Think of it, a homeowner owes a mortgage that is greater than what they could sell the house for. They get into trouble, fall behind and the bank starts to foreclose. The homeowner has none of their money in the house and simply gets up and leaves the property for the bank to get rid of.

I have seen it dozens of times and sat in many living rooms with homeowners who were unable to sell their home the conventional way. Heck, they couldn't even get a Realtor to talk to them since they could not list the property at a price they could pay the Realtor a commission. The homeowners are simply stuck. Unfortunately, many Realtors are either stuck in doing things the old way or just too darn lazy to learn how to help these property owners out of their financial mess. I will get into this later on in the book.

Most homeowners are very conscientious and want to do the right thing and pay the mortgage company or bank back, but they simply see no way out of their financial situation using the conventional means of selling their house. If they are smart enough to understand what it is that can be accomplished through the negotiation of reducing their debt with someone like me or a trained professional who understands the process, they do have a chance of getting out of the property without having a full blown foreclosure cloud their credit history.

With the advent of adjustable rate, interest only programs, reverse mortgages, zero down, no documentation, and other loan programs to numerous to mention out there, I have no doubt that we are only seeing the beginning of the foreclosure epidemic. I truly believe that this cycle will last at least until the end of 2010. It is a double-edged sword, as consumers we want these products and the providers of the financing are falling over themselves for your business. Something had to give, and it usually involves the bank taking the property back. It also creates a massive correction in the market in many areas of the country where the appreciation rates went through the roof.

❦ MAJOR REASONS FOR FORECLOSURE/DEFAULT ❦

Over the many years I have counseled homeowners, I have found that the major reasons people fall into default with their mortgages and eventually into foreclosure are varied. The main reasons are listed and explained below, in no particular order since if it is the reason you are in foreclosure; it is certainly the most important reason for your particular situation.

Job Loss / Income Decreases

This happens all the time, the couple living in the house qualified to buy the house based on two incomes. One income is lost or decreased and the juggling begins. If there is no rainy day fund, then even a temporary job loss of two to four months can be devastating. Since you must keep eating, paying the light and phone bills, the basic needs come first. It happened to me, the cost of my wife's medications were far more important than spending the money on the mortgage payment. If you have to make a choice between feeding your family and sending the money to the mortgage company, your family will always come first, as it should

I worked with a man who lost much of his business after the 911 attacks. He ran a home based consulting business and his income went from over $15,000 per month down to less than $2,000. His monthly mortgage payment was almost $3,000 and he had just refinanced his house to pay off his first wife. Nowhere to run and nowhere to hide, he was very much in a tough situation. We wound up selling his house for him and negotiating his second mortgage down from $128,000 to $25,000 in order to find a buyer.

Sickness

We have seen this situation many times with older couples where they have been working all their lives, they have older children and one of the wage earners becomes very ill with either a long-term sickness or a terminal condition. Their energy and resources are used to care for the sick family member and the mortgage falls behind.

Once again they are faced with tough choices if they have no funds in reserve. Again, we were involved with a middle-aged couple that had just adopted a special needs child when the wife's health began to deteriorate. The husband needed to care for his sick wife and care for the infant. The good news is the wife made a full recovery after about four months of being up and down, the bad news is that they were not able to keep the home from going into foreclosure. I hate it when bad things happen to very good people.

Adjustable Rate Mortgages

This reason is becoming more and more common. As a matter of fact this is becoming the main reason at this period of time in 2008 why there are so many properties in foreclosure. The weak dollar combined with the highest gas prices in history has stretched the budgets to a breaking point. When interest rates rise; some homeowners, whose mortgage interest rate is tied to the fluctuation of the prime lending rate, see their mortgage payments increase as well. If their income is not rising to meet the increase, or if the increase is too severe, it may cause them to fall behind.

They may have an option to re-finance to a fixed rate, if they are not hit with a pre-payment penalty that will force them to borrow more to payoff the original first. The margins may be so thin that they may not be able to qualify for a new loan and could be stuck with the adjustable rate loan. The banks and mortgage companies will usually only give you a month or two advanced warning that the increase is coming. Some do not even let you know; you just get your monthly statement and BAM your hit with an increase you did not see coming and you are financially unprepared to handle.

Divorce

This situation is much like a job loss or sickness when an income is lost due to dissolution of a marriage. We see numerous foreclosures that are caused by just this occurrence. The couple has qualified for the mortgage based on two incomes and one suddenly is no longer there. Many times the alimony or child support will pick up the slack, but we have found that when dealing with couples in the early stages or the middle of a divorce, it is sometimes better if the house is simply sold.

Banks and mortgage companies hate this scenario since they like to know they are dealing with both the husband and wife who signed the mortgage and not have to look all over the globe to serve them legal papers when the time comes if they have separated or vacated the home.

Relocating

For some reason, we see a lot of this situation here in Central Florida. Since Florida still draws a very transient population, there are many people who move down here, stay for a while and buy a house, they either miss family back where they came from originally, or can't stand the heat of the summers or the potential for hurricanes, and move back to where they came from.

Others are asked to relocate by their employer and must up and leave within a short time span. If the company they work for does not offer some sort of relocation assistance, then they are forced to move, many times without adequate time to sell the property before they move to another part of the country.

The problem arises when they are forced to make two monthly housing payments. I have been in this situation recently; this gets old very fast. Keep in mind that you still have to keep the lawn mowed and the property maintained. If this situation goes on for any length of time, they will fall behind on the property they have vacated.

100% or Over Financed

As I mentioned above when I blasted the banks and mortgage companies for creating this monster, this happens more times than I would care to admit. We are constantly negotiating debt off of over financed properties in order to get the homeowner out from under the problem. The banks and mortgage companies get ticked off that they have to discount the debt, but once they get the numbers back from their appraiser, they see they only have two choices.

The first choice is to accept our negotiated, discounted offer and get something for their loan balance right away. Or, they could foreclose and hope they recoup something after they have taken possession, done whatever repairs need to be done, paid insurance and property taxes on the property, pay a Realtor to help them sell it, and pay their attorney. More and more banks and mortgage companies are opting to deal with someone such as myself early in the process in order to minimize their cost of foreclosing, holding, and eventually disposing of the property.

Clearly that is good news for me and my associates as we are able to help more people get out from under their over leveraged house and make a fresh start. And since there are more and more people walking away from over-financed properties, the effect on neighborhoods has created a ripple in the basic market values of those neighborhoods.

Vacant House/Bad Tenants

The reason we list this separate is because we run across many investors who have had tenants who they had trouble getting out of their properties for non payment or the tenants made such a mess of the place, they decided to call it quits as a landlord. They were unable to keep this particular ball in the air, paying the mortgage on their own home while paying for an eviction and a mortgage on their investment property.

Bad tenants are the number one reason why investors throw in the towel and get out of the landlord business. Since many of my working years were spent in property management, this happens in both residential and commercial properties. It is very simple, if you are depending on a tenant to pay you so you can turn around and pay your mortgage company, the minute that tenant goes bad, you are still on the hook for the payment and the mortgage companies don't give a damn about your tenant from hell.

Another group of investors who got into the buying frenzy of a few years ago bought multiple properties on speculation that they could sell them quickly for a profit. Taking advantage of the rapid appreciation and turning a quick buck. Some were very successful and made some money because they got in early. Others who got in at the tail end were left holding the bag when properties stopped selling quickly and the appreciation rates began to top out or decline. Many of these "investors" tapped into their home equity lines of credit to purchase these properties. Now not only are they losing their investment properties, they have put their primary residences at risk.

Many investors with multiple properties can weather this storm. However, I have worked with numerous clients who had just that one investment property and had problems with a tenant who wound up either losing the property or coming very close. I have enclosed a copy of a nice letter I received from a single mom who went through this exact problem that we were able to help out. See the end of this chapter the testimonial letters we received from a few property owners we were able to help.

Owe Liens / Estates

Many homeowners incur liens that are attached to the property, making it almost impossible to sell. If these liens are from the federal, state, or local government such the IRS, state income tax, or local property taxes, then your property may become so burdened by non-mortgage debt that it may not be worth your time to stay in the house and continue to pay the mortgage. Tradesman who have performed work on your house, but have never been paid can also place liens on your property. They have the right to lien or attach a lien on your property that will force you to pay them off when the time comes for you to sell.

There will be greater discussion on this topic later when we discuss some strategies for getting these off your property.

There have been many instances where properties with mortgages still unpaid were part of an estate. If the beneficiaries do not or cannot continue to keep the mortgage paid and current, the bank will foreclose, regardless if the borrower is dead or alive.

Fire Damage / Storm Damage / Needs Repairs

We have seen this situation constantly here in Central Florida. A few years ago we experienced three hurricanes in Central Florida that simply devastated areas of the state. Many homeowners who were unable to get their homes repaired after their insurance settlement check arrived due to a higher than normal deductible are forced with either giving up their home and selling it for what they could, or borrowing money to make the needed repairs.

This situation happens with investors as well. When a property owner owns a property that is in obvious need of repairs, they have only two choices; fix the problem or sell the house at the discounted price.

When homeowners can't make the repairs, the home becomes more susceptible to damage and loss of value. When the homeowner is making payments on a home that is in disrepair, they are more apt to up and leave and not deal with the needed repairs. If a bank is made aware of this situation and they are willing to work with a homeowner, the homeowner may have found a solution to saving their home.

❧ POTENTIAL SOURCES TO KEEP YOUR SHIP AFLOAT ❧

Please pay close attention to what will follow and heed my warnings that the short-term solutions I am about to discuss are not a cure all. Since I did not have a long-term plan for repayment set up with the bank, my first option was to draw on every credit line I had via some credit cards. It was not the smartest thing I could have done, but I really wasn't thinking very clearly.

If you plan on making up the back amounts due to the mortgage company, also keep in mind that if you are three months behind on your payments, chances are you have a couple of hundred dollars in additional late fees tacked on to the regular payment amounts. If the bank has initiated the foreclosure action, you should also expect to pay for the banks attorney fees as well.

If you do decide to bring the loan current, or in bank terms, "cure the default", please get the exact dollar figure you will need from either someone at the bank or through the attorney handling the case for the bank. The figure they will give you will have an expiration date and after that date, the amount due will have to be recalculated.

Always send certified funds and always send the payment in a fashion where you can confirm it was received. Either, certified, return receipt requested from the post office or anyone of the overnight delivery services like FedEx and UPS.

Now that you know what and how to send the payment, here are a few sources where you can get these funds:

Borrow on Your Home Equity

This option may or may not be available for a couple of reasons. The first being that if you are seriously behind on your first mortgage, many companies simply will not write a new loan if the first mortgage is in default. If you think that re-financing might be an option, this same situation will arise when you try that avenue as well. Be careful of predatory lenders out there who will take advantage of your desperate situation and charge you higher than normal points, fees, and interest rates if you are able to get re-financing.

Most of the three big credit reporting bureaus will quickly pick up the negative credit information from your lender. This occurrence usually will result in an immediate drop in your credit score. Be aware of it.

If you do have an equity credit line in place already, and you are able to tap into it before the foreclosure is filed, then there is a real opportunity to avert the foreclosure. Your payments on the amount borrowed from the equity credit line is usually much lower since the interest rates on equity lines of credit are historically much lower than credit card cash advances. Just know what you are getting into and if the additional payments you will be making fit into your now revised budget.

Credit Card Credit Lines

If you recall, this is how I funded our living expenses while we were headed to foreclosure. I could not bring the amounts due current with the credit cards I had, since many were already carrying huge balances. I would never suggest that you go this route; this is a recipe for disaster in the long run. But if it comes down to food, medication, or other vital expenditures, then use what you have available.

If you are just a month or two behind and your cash flow problems are temporary, then I see no reason not to use this as a sort of loan. I am constantly getting these balance transfer checks all the time in the mail. Why couldn't you use these funds to get caught up? Although the interest rates are usually very high, it is better than having a 30, 60, or 90-day late notice appear on your credit report from your mortgage company.

Only you will know what you can and cannot do regarding this option. Just be careful you are not digging yourself a larger, deeper hole that will be very difficult if not impossible to get out. Like I said before, I do not advise people to do this unless they are certain they know what they are getting into.

Tap Pension or 401K Plans

I have come across a couple of homeowners who have done just this especially when they were transferred and were unable to keep up with two house payments until their old house was sold. They simply tapped into or cashed into their pension plans from their old employer in some way and kept that money as a reserve fund to pay the mortgage. Since I have never worked for a company that offered a pension plan, I have no idea as to the logistics of all this, I have just spoken to and interviewed people who have taken advantage of this funding source. It is certainly not recommended you tap into retirement funds; however we are talking about taking desperate measures to save your home and credit.

Keep in mind that there may also be tax implications by going this route since there are penalties for early withdrawals from pension and 401K plans. Again, this is a great example and case for having Accounting and Financial professionals assist you with this as the tax consequences are way out of my realm of knowledge. This will be a decision only you can make given your tax situation.

Relatives or Friends

When we were paying the trustee during our bankruptcy, I had to borrow $5,000.00 from my wife's uncle. He was gracious and kind enough to lend us the money for our short-term crunch, but I also paid him back first as soon as we could. This may be a viable option to many people experiencing a short-term squeeze in income. As long as the friends and relatives understand what the problem is and when they will be getting their money back, it is a good solid option.

Many times family members will allow you a low or no interest arrangement. I know it took a lot of swallowing of my bruised pride to ask, but looking back now, it was absolutely the right thing to do. I also made darn sure Uncle Mitch was paid back, every penny and some interest I insisted on paying him.

Although your financial position may feel somewhat embarrassing to you, it certainly was for me so I know what you are going through. However, it may be the only way to get back on your feet. Don't be too proud to ask for help, you may be surprised by the response you get. As long as you have never made a habit of borrowing money from relatives in the past, and if you did, paid them back in full, you should seriously consider this as an option.

Sell Assets

Another solid strategy for rounding up some capital is selling off some of the "stuff" you have accumulated over the years. I know of one young couple that had fallen behind on their mortgage and were beginning to drown in a sea of debt. The young couple had two vehicles, both late model cars that were about 50% paid for. I suggested since they worked in the same office park, but reported to work only a half hour apart that they sell off one of the cars and start commuting together to the office every morning.

It was like the obvious solution to a short-term money problem that it never dawned on them. Will this work for every situation, probably not. Their problem was deciding who's car to get rid of, I would have love to be a fly on the wall during that decision.

We also worked with another couple that was falling behind a payment or two and as I walked into their home, this big screen TV was the size of a movie screen. We later learned it was fully paid for and worth about $3,500, just enough to get them out of the hole. Boy was that guy ticked off at me for suggesting they sell that and get caught up. Just keep an open mind and determine what is more important, the "stuff" in the house or the house that contains it.

Talk to Bank or Mortgage Company Early

As time goes on, Loss Mitigation departments are getting involved earlier and earlier in the default process. If they are made aware of your short-term cash problems early in the process, many times they will offer help or assistance right away.

We will get into much greater detail later on in this book with examples of forbearance agreements and what to ask and say to the people in the Loss Mitigation departments to try and get what you want. You should always try and keep the lines of communication open, no matter how vicious and adversarial the relationship gets with the people in other departments of the bank or mortgage company. Just because the people on the other end of the line are being jerks, don't drop down to their level. Keep it civil and you will get better results.

The next chapter will deal with Mortgages, Liens, and other debt that can be placed on your property and how to deal with it all.

TESTIMONIAL LETTERS FROM PEOPLE WE HAVE ASSISTED

Dear Clyde:

I want to thank you for all you have done for me. I don't know what I would have done if you hadn't stepped in when I was having so much trouble with my tenants. You got them out and even now people are still calling and looking for them. If you had not helped me I would have lost everything. God sent you when I needed you most.

I just knew I could trust you from the time we met.

I'm still trying to work this computer; I hope this gets to you.

My love to you and your wife.

Thank you.

Margaret Wolford
Eustice, Florida

Clyde Goulet
P.O. Box 953085
Lake Mary, Florida 32795

Dear Mr. Goulet

We are sending this letter to express how much we enjoyed working with you. We had never heard of anyone helping prevent foreclosure before, so we were a little apprehensive. When we met with you, our fears were immediately put to rest because of your knowledge and ability to explain the process and convey the information so that it was easily understood. We were at the point of losing our house and in less than three months you had our house sold.

You have our complete appreciation and admiration. We would and have recommended you to everyone we can.

Sincerely,
John & Tara Longway
Debary, Florida

Mr. Clyde Goulet
C/O Lake Mary Realty, Inc.
P.O. Box 953085
Lake Mary, Florida 32795

Re: 103 Edgewater Circle, Sanford

Dear Clyde,

We both wanted to stop and write you a quick thank you note for handling the property in Sanford. The entire transaction from start to finish could not have gone any smoother that it was.

It is rare indeed in this day and age when businesses and people do exactly what they have promised to do. Both you Clyde and Lake Mary Realty did everything you promised you were going to do and we thank you and wish you continued success in helping property owners out of difficult situations.

We thank you for your honesty and integrity and will look for opportunities to send clients your way in the future. Thanks again for your assistance.

Very Truly Yours,
Robert & Peggy Sinclaire
Pierson, Florida

* You can sign up for a FREE e-course about the Foreclosure process at:
www.clydegoulet.com

Chapter 3

Mortgages, Liens, Judgments, Etc.

❧ WHAT EXACTLY ARE WE SIGNING AND HOW DOES IT IMPACT OUR LIVES. ❧

I must be perfectly honest and candid, even though I have been in the real estate business for many years; I never fully understood the many details of the mortgage and notes we signed when we purchased a property. I guess I was just too lazy to read all the paragraphs and clauses in the document that was to become a major problem for me down the road. A document that leads me to understand what rights we have as consumers and what rights the originator of the mortgage and note actually had.

This chapter will go through in detail exactly what this document is as well as what your legal rights are. We will also discuss the abuses of banks and mortgage companies when enforcing this document. Also, how to protect your best interest and know for certain, in general terms your rights and responsibilities. We will also get into the hierarchy of the loan/lien structure and display in detail who the players that are in this drama and who it is that carries the biggest stick when it comes time to collect their debts. After reading this chapter, it is my hope that you will be more than adequately armed to handle any call from a junior lien holder who is making your life miserable.

❧ THE MORTGAGE & NOTE ❧

As defined by Webster's dictionary: <u>Mortgage,</u> *a conveyance of property (as for security on a loan) on condition that the conveyance becomes void on payment or performance according to stipulated terms.*

The mortgage is a separate and distinct document that is signed along with the Promissory Note at the closing table. The mortgage simply conveys or transfers the property over to you the new owner. The promissory note contains the wording of your payment plan and is defined in the dictionary as such:

Promissory Note, *a written promise to pay at a fixed or determinable future time a sum of money to a specific individual or bearer.*

Take the time to read the definitions, there is a vast difference in what each is designed to accomplish for the lender making the loan. In this day and age, the time when a mortgage was given by the local community bank and stayed at that bank are over. Mortgages are commodities that are bought and sold like mutual funds buy and sell stocks. There are financial institutions that devote a large portion of their business to buying and selling blocks or pools of mortgages.

We have seen just recently that the companies making policy and funding these loans with the backing of the Federal Government have come under serious scrutiny. We have even seen top executives be indicted regarding the types of mortgages that were allowed to be bought and sold. There is even speculation that the people in these companies knew of the high risk of these mortgage pools and did not guard against the potential wide spread defaults that resulted from the lax credit policies.

In the easiest of explanation about these mortgage backed securities let me explain the various levels of mortgage debt. There are institutional buyers of "A" & "B" paper or loans made to people with outstanding to good credit and there is "C" & "D" mortgages that are bought and sold that carry more risk for the buyers because they are loans to people with less than perfect credit or mortgages with high loan to value ratios. The bottom line is the company that originated your loan is very likely not the company servicing your loan.

I know in my situation our loan on the house we lived in for ten years was bought and sold at least four times in ten years. In one particular change over they lost one of our payments and it caused a problem for about three months until it was recovered.

❧ THE BORROWERS RESPONSIBILITY ❧

Clearly the main responsibility you have as the borrower is to pay the loan back within the time specified and make the payments on time. In many notes and mortgages you will be required to show proof of having adequate insurance coverage naming the bank or mortgage company as the loss payee in case of loss of value on the property due to some sort of damage.

The bank or mortgage company also has the right to force place insurance on your property without your permission to protect their interest. You really should try and avoid this ever happening since the insurance they force place on your property is usually two to three times more expensive than if you would have paid for it yourself and shopped around for the lowest quote.

In most cases you will also be required to pay your real estate taxes on a timely basis or face the potential for the bank to force you to create an escrow account for these funds. I always allow them to withhold and escrow funds for this purpose, but I do watch the balance very closely as the banks have a tendency to over withhold funds and in essence you are giving them an interest free loan on the excess funds.

Since your first and primary responsibility is to pay the first mortgage holder, they have inserted some clauses into the language of the note that stipulates that if payments are not made, they have the right to accelerate the loan and call it due and payable in full. In a nuts and bolts example, this is exactly what a mortgage foreclosure is, the bank exercising their right under the acceleration clause to call the debt due in full in order to take back control of the property.

THE BANKS/MORTGAGE COMPANY'S RESPONSIBILITY

Besides the obvious responsibility of collecting the payments and making sure your payments are credited properly regarding the amounts to pay interest, principal, and escrow. They also have a responsibility to whom ever they are servicing the loan for to make sure the loan is in what they call a "performing state". Non-performing loans are loans in default or in foreclosure.

The company servicing the loan will enforce all the provisions of the note and besides having the right to accelerate the loan, also have the ability to work with the borrower. Not only do they have the right to work with the borrower, they have an obligation to do so. Please allow me a brief stroll back in history.

Back in the late eighties and early nineties the Federal Government had to step in and form a government agency called the Resolution Trust Company/Corporation or RTC. The RTC was commissioned to assist all the banks and mortgage institutions that wrote billions of dollars in bad loans with the task of disposing of millions of dollars worth of properties, both residential and commercial. Since many of these loans were backed by the federal government via the Fannie Mae, Freddie Mac, HUD, and other programs available at the time, the RTC took over many of the savings and loan companies and liquidated their loan portfolios at pennies on the dollar. In other words, they foreclosed on the properties and sold the properties to investors at huge losses, all absorbed by the taxpayers of the country. That means you and me baby!

In order to try and insure this never happened again, the federal government demanded that any bank or mortgage company lending federally backed funds for mortgages, and most all do, establish a department in the bank to help with the workout of troubled loans and they wound up being called either the "Workout" or "Loss Mitigation" departments. Their primary job is to try and work with the borrower to avert the foreclosure from ever happening. Chapter 5 will explain in detail the process of dealing with the Loss Mitigation departments and we will get into specific examples of what they do and how they can help you.

❧ COMMON MISCONCEPTIONS ABOUT MORTGAGES ❧

I have been told by numerous clients that the trained gorillas working in the collection department of the bank would threaten them saying that they will come after them personally if they do not pay and attach checking accounts and other bull. The fact of the matter is the only collateral the bank has, in almost every case, for the mortgage is the physical property itself. In other words, if they are forced to foreclose, their only recourse against you the borrower is to take the property back and resell the property to recoup their unpaid mortgage balance and hopefully their attorney fees as well. They cannot put you in jail or garnish wages. They can only look to the property as collateral for the loan balance.

If the loan was obtain through fraudulent means, for instance an inflated appraisal or if you the borrower lied on the loan application, then the appraiser could find themselves in trouble and you could be subject to some questions if not legal actions as well. I have seen instances where both the mortgage broker and appraiser were working in tandem to inflate values and misstate income in order to get the loans approved. Just know whom you are dealing with.

The vast majority of home loans do not carry with them a personal guarantee by the borrower to repay. As stated above, the only collateral or recourse the bank has is the property. They will try and bully people by stating that they have the right to come after other assets but in reality they can only take the house back. If the property is foreclosed and they are forced to resell it, they may come after you for what is called a deficiency judgment. The judgment is for the difference between what was owed, including attorney fees minus what they were able to sell the property for. (* See the end of this chapter for an update on this topic and how it may impact you.)

I have found that many banks will not do this for the simple reason it takes too much time and energy to keep the records on these and they simply write the losses off. Even when we have negotiated Short Sale payoffs for homeowners, we have insisted they waive their right for a deficiency judgment as part of the contract and they have agreed. Bottom line is, it is not cast in stone and as things currently stand is very rarely enforced. That doesn't mean that you should not protect yourself and guard against it becoming an issue.

Another common misconception regarding foreclosures is that when you are served with your notice of foreclosure, you must begin to vacate the property. The legal term is the Lis Pendens notice; this is just stating the bank intends to bring legal action to foreclose. You continue to have the rights of homeownership up until the property is sold on the courthouse steps and in most states we are talking months, not weeks. Then you will have a certain amount of time to vacate and this time frame varies from state to state.

As this update is written in the early summer of 2008 there have been many changes in the timelines. What has happened is that the shear volume of the foreclosures that must be worked through the civil court system is slowing the process down to a crawl.

What used to take a few months to get moving through the courts is now pushing out as long as four to six months. I have spoken to people who are as much as eight months behind on their mortgages and have yet to be served their notices of default from the court indicating that a foreclosure action has begun by their lender.

At all times during this legal process you have the right to cure the default and bring the loan current. In effect by bringing the loan current, allowing you to reinstate the loan to the status of current in the eyes of the bank. I have heard stories of people at the bank telling customers they will be physically dragged from their house if they do not pay up by a certain date and that if they did not pay a certain amount by a specified time they would not have the right to reinstate the loan somewhere down the line. These comments are simply not true and are used in an effort to intimidate.

My final suggestion on this topic is to take the time to find the wording on reinstatement in your mortgage document and become aware of your rights. Since every mortgage document has subtle differences, it would be difficult to say they are all treated the same. Look it up and go through it, you do have the right to bring it current no matter how far you are behind. As far as time goes, you can wait until the day the foreclosure is set to take place on the courthouse steps and if you have the full amount available to pay the back payments, late fees, attorney fees, and other crap fess tacked on by the bank, you can stop the foreclosure and reinstate the loan. I don't suggest you cut it that close though, better to be safe than sorry. Know your rights; you have more options than you know.

THE LOAN HIERARCHY

You should also know that not all loans are created equally. In the case of mortgages attached to property, the mortgage that is first in line carries most of the clout. This does not mean to say that the second mortgage holder cannot foreclose; they most certainly can and will in some cases. It simply means that the process is more difficult for a second mortgage holder, as we will get into now.

What constitutes a first or second mortgage? It is simply determined by what mortgage lien gets recorded first at the county courthouse. On some rare occasions when a recorder or Title Company messed up the order or recording, it usually does not happen, but if it were to happen, it could cause a large mess somewhere down the road. The reason for the importance of who gets first position and what mortgage or lien gets relegated to the junior positions are basically two fold.

If a first mortgage holder proceeds with a foreclosure action and completes the process and the property is sold on the courthouse steps, all junior liens are wiped out, that is the first important reason for being in the primary position. The implications are that the first mortgage holder can now sell this property minus all other encumbrances. If the property winds up selling for much greater than the first mortgage balance, the junior lien holders may get some of their money from the excess funds.

You may be thinking why anyone would loan money and take on a junior position? The reason comes down to the perceived equity in the property and the risk the second mortgage lenders are willing to take. Keep in mind the second mortgage rates are usually substantially higher than first mortgage rates, so don't feel too bad for them. They market hot and heavy to anyone who may have some equity and loan the money freely and some times easily, they are willing to live with the risk in an appreciating market and with the higher interest rates they charge.

With the relative flood of the 80/20 loan combinations out there, the 20% second mortgages are everywhere. It was a very popular financing product for the builders of the many new subdivisions being constructed and brought many more potential buyers into the market.

Since they are in the second position, the only way they would be able to avoid being wiped out at a foreclosure of the first mortgage is to show up at the courthouse steps at the foreclosure sale and completely pay off the first mortgage, including all the late fees, attorney fees and other junk fees tacked on. Once this is done, their second mortgage now bumps to the first position and they in essence own the property.

The second mortgage holder now becomes the first mortgage holder and owner of the property enabling them to dispose of the property in the hopes of getting their money back. This is all very good in theory, but does this actually happen and is a second mortgage holder willing to put up the kind of money to secure their second mortgage position? Most won't, some will and to follow are a couple of examples to look over.

Keep in mind before you look these over that each of these examples is not unusual or out of the ordinary. I have seen representatives for many second mortgage holders refuse to believe that they would get wiped out if the first mortgage foreclosed. When you take into account the people I dealt with did not know the detail of the mortgage documents, their ignorance was really not their own fault. They were simply acting as collection agents and were simply not aware that all their huffing and puffing they were doing was actually kind of comical. I knew them being in the second mortgage position was not good and they were in deep fertilizer and had no easy way to tell them they were wrong and they would end up losing their money if and when the first mortgage foreclosed.

Here is that example:

Facts of the case:

Home Market Value:	$ 150,000.00
First Mortgage Balance: (Including Late Fees, Attorney Fees, Back Taxes)	$ 139,575.00
Second Mortgage Balance	$ 18,000.00

Would it make sense for the second mortgage holder to pay off the first mortgage at the courthouse steps to protect their position? What would they "net" after all is said and done?

Mortgages, Liens, Judgments, Etc.

Sell Home For Market Value:	$ 150,000.00
Less: Payoff of First Mortgage	- 139,575.00
Less: Real Estate Commission (6%)	- 9,000.00
Net To Second Mortgage Holder:	$ 1,425.00

There is no company in the world that would do this given these numbers. I have seen these almost exact numbers many times and this is where we have been able to help homeowners negotiate debt down on both the first and second mortgages. If you take a hard look at the numbers for the first mortgage holder, they may be happy getting $125,000 for their first mortgage since there is no guarantee that they will get the full $150,000 market value when they sell the property after they have been awarded the title after the foreclosure. They will also have to pay a sales commission when selling through a Realtor, reducing their "net" even greater.

When you compound this with the fact that there are holding costs such as insurance, real estate taxes, homeowners association fees, landscaping, and the list could go on, depending on where the property is located. When they factor into the equation what their real "net" from the deal might end up being, they most likely will work the Short Sale.

The bottom line is that with someone actively negotiating on your behalf running these numbers for the first and second mortgage holders will in most cases open their eyes as to what they will actually net somewhere down the line. It is a business decision for them and if we can convince them the numbers we are giving them make sense; they will discount their mortgages and work with us on Short Sale deals.

If that first mortgage in the above example had a balance of only $80,000, the second mortgage holder showing up at the courthouse steps would have made perfect sense. There would have been more than enough equity for them to get back the $80,000 they shell out for the first and recover the $18,000 they have into the deal.

The reason for this lengthy discussion of what happens with the first and second mortgages is to let you know who is carrying the biggest stick. You should never be intimidated by a second mortgage holder anymore. They are in just as bad a position as you are if you are in default with the first mortgage holder. You may be surprised to know that some second mortgage holders don't even know the first mortgage holder has begun to foreclose and that they are in jeopardy of getting wiped out if the property is sold at the courthouse steps. I have found that companies in the second position become very willing to get something out of their mortgage, even if it is 10 cents on the dollar. 10% of something is better than 100% of nothing.

The second mortgage holder may huff and puff and threaten to blow your house in, but all they carry is a lot of hot air. Educate them, keep all conversations civil since you may come back later asking for a discount and you never want to burn bridges. Threats by them will accomplish nothing if you know who has the power in the mortgage hierarchy. It will serve you in the long run to know who has the most leverage in your particular case.

❦ NEGOTIATING FOR DISCOUNTS ❦

As I mentioned above, out of chaos comes some opportunity. If you have been having some short term money problems and you have a first and second mortgage both in default and are able to come up with some money and can bring the first current, before you do that approach the second mortgage holder and ask if they would be interested in taking a discount on their second mortgage. You may get a very negative response at first or an offer of 50% to 75% of the total debt, but remember their position. I would have no problem telling them if the property goes to the foreclosure sale at the courthouse steps they will be wiped out. If they are aware of the foreclosure, they will at least listen to you.

The same holds true for any liens or judgments that have been attached to the property. Many lien holders like tradesman and companies who have placed the liens on the property will be happy to take something, anything; if they are informed the property will be foreclosed on. You may want to send them a copy of the initial notice of foreclosure as proof. Sometimes the junior lien holders are all notified when the first mortgage holder is foreclosing. The second mortgage holder is almost always notified, not always the case for lien and judgment holders.

As part of my business, I am constantly getting liens and judgments removed from properties and helping homeowners sell their over encumbered properties. The process takes some time and there is paperwork involved that must be signed, sometimes notarized, and always recorded on public record. If you are able to get debt taken off your property, you want to make sure that fact becomes public record.

✲ IRS LIENS ✲

A full discussion of liens and judgments would not be complete unless our friends at the IRS were not mentioned. When it comes to the rule that all liens and judgments are stacked behind the first and second mortgage, well the rules change when the IRS is involved. You see they get to leap frog over all other liens and judgments and get paid if there are excess funds after the first mortgage is paid. The good news in this situation is that if you can show proof to the IRS that there would be insufficient funds to pay them from the closing of the real estate transaction, they will allow your request to remove the lien from the property allowing you to transfer clear title to the new owners.

Now since I originally wrote the paragraph above I have been challenged a couple of times whether that information is accurate. Since I do not keep up with the thousands of changes to the tax code every year, I will not dispute their claims nor will I spend time figuring out what the IRS does anymore. I will tell you to check with your Accountant or CPA about the consequences of having the IRS attach their lien to your property. What I have been told is that if the lien cannot be satisfied by the equity in the property, then the lien continues to be attached to the individuals personally. I can't see the IRS operating in any other way.

I always thought that an IRS lien was like a tattoo, once you have one it stays with you until you have it taken off. I was always under the impression that the IRS does allow you to dispose of a property but retain the IRS lien on your personal record. Again, check with someone who is trained and keeps up with the constant changes in tax code and the IRS circus. If my information is incorrect, take this as my official disclaimer. I never said I had ALL the answers.

❧ FINAL THOUGHTS ❧

I realize some of this information can be dull and boring, however if you are to protect your self-interest you must know how the system works and the opportunities you have to save yourself some money or get out from under the mountain of debt. In chapter 8 I will make the case for and against filing for bankruptcy, with no personal gain in the matter and from someone who has been through one. My opinions may be biased, but I have also taken the arrows and I am still standing here trying to help and educate as many people who will stop long enough to listen.

Regardless of how bleak the situation may look if you are facing multiple mortgages, liens, and judgments on your property that are in default, you should now know that basically everything is negotiable. Take advantage of the opportunity to have the debt discounted off of the property. You really have nothing to lose simply by asking.

❧ HOUSE RESOLUTION # 3648 ❧

** Here is some rather good news on the mortgage foreclosure front. Although it is not a permanent change to the IRS code, it does open a window for a few people anyway. This H.R. # 3648 was passed into law on January 4th of this year and will sunset or expires at midnight December 31, 2009.

The basic wording, under the provisions and guidelines described in the IRS code stated that in the past, before HR 3648 the IRS would treat discharged or forgiven debt as taxable income. I have copied this resolution, at least the section that pertains to the people reading this book that it may effect in an effort for you to have it at your disposal to take to your Accountant or CPA if they have not become aware of this change as of yet. I hope that you find it helpful, if you can wade through the legalese.

One Hundred Tenth Congress
Of The
United States Of America

AT THE FIRST SESSION

Begun and held at the City of Washington,

The fourth day of January, two thousand and seven

An Act

To amend the Internal Revenue Code of 1986 to exclude discharge of indebtedness on principal residences from gross income, and for other purposes.

Be it enacted by the Senate and House of Representatives of the United States of America in Congress assembled,

SECTION 1. SHORT TITLE.

This Act may be cited as the "Mortgage Forgiveness Debt Relief Act of 2007".

SECTION 2. DISCHARGES OF INDEBTEDNESS ON PRINCIPAL RESIDENCE EXCLUDED FROM GROSS INCOME.

(a)   In General – Paragraph (1) of section 108(a) of the Internal Revenue Code of 1986 is amended by striking 'or' at the end of subparagraph (C), by striking the period at the end of subparagraph (D) and inserting, 'or', and by inserting after subparagraph (D) the following new subparagraph:

'(E) the indebtedness discharged is qualified principal residence Indebtedness which is discharged before January 1, 2010.'.

(b) Special Rules Relating to Qualified Principal Residence Indebtedness – Section 108 of such Code is amended by adding at the end the following new subsection:

(h) Special Rules Relating to Qualified Principal Residence Indebtedness-

(1) BASIS REDUCTION- The amount excluded from gross income by reason of subsection (a)(1)(E) shall be applied to reduce (but not below zero) the basis of the principal residence of the taxpayer.

(2) QUALIFIED PRINCIPAL RESIDENCE INDEBTEDNESS- For purposes of this section, the term 'qualified principal residence indebtedness' means acquisition indebtedness (within the meaning of section 163(h)(3)(B), applied by substituting '$2,000,000 ($1,000,000' for '$1,000,000 ($500,000' in clause (ii) thereof) with respect to the principal residence of the taxpayer.

(3) EXCEPTION FOR CERTAIN DISCHARGES NOT RELATED TO TAXPAYER'S FINANCIAL CONDITION- Subsection (a)(1)(E) shall not apply to the discharge of a loan if the discharge is on account of services performed for the lender or any other factor not directly related to a decline in the value of the residence or to the financial condition of the taxpayer.

(4) ORDERING RULE- If any loan is discharged, in whole or in part, and only a portion of such loan is qualified principal residence indebtedness, subsection (a)(1)(E) shall apply only to so much of the amount discharged as exceeds the amount of the loan (as determined immediately before such discharge) which is not qualified principal residence indebtedness.

(5) PRINCIPAL RESIDENCE- For purposes of this subsection, the term 'principal residence' has the same meaning as when used in section 121.

(c) Coordination-

(1) Subparagraph (A) of section 108(a)(2) of such Code is amended by striking 'and (D)' and inserting '(D), and (E)'.

(2) Paragraph (2) of section 108(a) of such Code is amended by adding at the end the following new subparagraph:

(C) PRINCIPAL RESIDENCE EXCLUSION TAKES PRE-CEDENCE OVER INSOLVENCY EXCLUSION UNLESS ELECTED OTHERWISE- Paragraph (1)(B) shall not apply to a discharge to which paragraph (1)(E) applies unless the taxpayer elects to apply paragraph (1)(B) in lieu of paragraph (1)(E).

(d) Effective Date- The amendments made by this section shall apply to discharges of indebtedness on or after January 1, 2007.

There you have it; the "sweeping" changes will expire at midnight on December 31, 2009. Your debt gets discharged after that, sorry pal you're flat out of luck. This of course applies only to your principal residence.

Of course the geniuses in Washington wouldn't think of making this permanent, that would make much too much sense and would give the people who need the break the most an actual break. Is it any wonder why people have such little faith in government these days to do the right thing when given the opportunity?

I could spend another ten pages dumping on the pin heads in Washington D.C. but that is not why you are reading this book. I hope the above reference will be of some assistance. We will move on to the next chapter.

Chapter 4

Confrontation 101 – Or Dealing With The Trained Gorillas In The Collections Department

❧ A GUIDE OF WHAT TO EXPECT AND HOW TO DEAL WITH THE STRESS. ❧

There was nothing in my life that quite prepared me for what I went through when the various collection departments began calling on the loans and credit cards we were delinquent on. As the time went by the calls became more and more vicious in their tone and being usually a very reserved person who has always been kind of laid back until pushed into a corner, it was a rude awakening, in more ways than one.

I guess since I have been through the whole foreclosure gambit from start to finish, I think I am more than qualified to comment on what I think crosses the line and what would constitute acceptable business practices. I can say without doubt or reserve that some of the behavior I was subjected to from the collections department bordered on harassment.

I certainly understand that they are just doing their jobs. Their job is to extract as much money out of you as humanly or inhumanly as possible in the shortest period of time. Since I do not know how they are paid, I must assume they are paid hourly and have no financial interest if they collect all or a portion of the past due amounts they are calling you on. In other words, I don't think they are paid a commission of any kind of compensation on the amount of money they get customers to fork over.

Since their primary job is to extract any amount of money out of you, they will do and say just about anything to get this money. Since I am relaying to you personal experiences, I have no idea if the tactics used on me where company policy or strictly the modus operandi of the particular mortgage company that was hammering me up one side and down the other. I know that after each one of these confrontations I wanted to punch a wall.

❦ THE COLLECTION CYCLE ❦

The official collection calls can usually begin after being behind 30 days. If you have been late a couple of months making your payment, they may begin in the middle of the month of the same month your payment is due. But as a general rule, if your payment was due on say March 1, and April 1 rolls around, expect to start getting calls on a regular basis. At first these calls will ask you to call their customer service for an important message, sometimes the message is left by a live operator and sometimes it will be computer generated.

There have been many changes since the above paragraph was written. I know that there is a greater period of time that now elapses before the calls begin. I know this from speaking to my clients and others going through foreclosure or have fallen way behind and have yet to receive a single call or notification.

As I stated earlier, the backlog is simply overwhelming for some of these lenders as they are having trouble keeping up with the cases they have that have already been initiated by their attorneys. There is a good news/bad news situation here. The good news is that these long delays are allowing much more time to work out Short Sale deals. The bad news is that the payment clock is always ticking and the amounts not paid will need to be accounted for and paid back or restructured in some way, shape, or form.

If they are successful in reaching you, they will be somewhat cordial for the most part asking when the last payment that was due will be paid. They will ask you for a date certain in which you will be sending the payment. Currently they are able to accept checks by phone. When we went through our foreclosure, this option was not available to the mortgage company. They may ask you to send the payment via overnight mail or other traceable means of delivery.

Confrontation 101 – Or Dealing With The Trained Gorillas

I would not suggest giving any company the routing numbers and account numbers of your checking account. I know they can only take what you have agreed to send, but the thought of any company having this information available to them just leaves a bad taste in my mouth. Better to be safe then sorry, this is another reason I do not allow any business or company to have an automatic draft from my checking account.

When you begin to hit the 60-day period of delinquency, under normal circumstances the calls generally will be more frequent and escalate in tone. They will call every night and on weekends as well until they reach someone live. If you get tired of explaining to them you are working towards a solution or just don't want the headaches, just get an answering machine and screen your calls.

No matter what you tell them at this point they will be looking to get you to send some kind of payment to them as soon as possible. I remember a conversation I had with a particular person when we were 60 days behind and was so ticked off, it kept me up that night. When I told the horses rear end on the other end of the line that I had a choice of either sending a partial payment to the mortgage company or purchasing prescriptions for my wife and that the mortgage company would have to wait. The guy on the other end of the line suggested that my wife wait and we send them whatever we had even if it meant going without life's necessities.

I wanted to rip the guys' lungs out through the phone. It was from that moment on that I lost any real motivation to work with the mortgage company in any way. That conversation so turned me off to that mortgage company that every time one of them called after that date I was as rude as I could be, despite given the fact that I grew up in a good Christian home. I never used profanities, but I knew I would never send them another dime. In hind sight, I would never do that again as it really closed off any opportunity I might have had to work out a solution that would have benefited me and my wife. I let emotions get in the way of doing what was best for me and my family.

Another aspect of the collection process that really bothered me early on was that you never spoke to the same person twice. If you had developed rapport with one person, you would never hear from them again. Makes no sense to me why they run their business like this. One of the reasons why this tends to happen is because there is such a huge turnover in these call centers that they either don't last on the job or get promoted to another department.

When the clock reaches the 90-day or three months delinquent phase, the collection calls continue with the same frequency and they begin trying to reach you via every phone number you may have. If you are working and have given them your work number, they will call you there and confront you while you work. I know of one person who was called so often at work, he nearly lost his job on account of it. Imagine the irony, working to make up the past due mortgage payments and the mortgage company costing you your job because of the persistent phone calls.

If you give them a cell phone number, they will call that as well. If they do not have your direct number, but have a close relatives phone number, they will call them and ask that you call them as soon as possible. They are brazen and relentless in their attempt to contact you. If you get fed up with the constant calls and begin to feel overly stressed, it would not hurt to either change your phone number or simply don't answer the phone.

I say this only if you are not pursuing a remedy to get your back amount paid up and or save your home. If you are working with the bank and have made arrangements to get caught up, it is imperative that you keep the lines of communication open at all times. The price you pay for this is the occasional rude call from a member of the collections department that may have called you and does not know you are working with them to make payments.

Although they all have access to the same information in their computer systems, there is always a call from an idiot who does not read the data in their system and is making the usual bullying call. Always try and get the names of the people you talk to as well as the date and time. When you do get that call, you can reference the name of the person you spoke to and the day you last talked. I have always found this to be extremely helpful especially when I am negotiating the debt down for a client of mine. This information will be in the bank or Mortgage Company's computer system and then the jerk that called can go back and see that you are in fact working with someone.

Confrontation 101 – Or Dealing With The Trained Gorillas

❧ TRUE LIES ❧

You must always remember to take whatever is being said by the people in the collections department with a grain of salt. What they say maybe true in the long run, but they themselves have no power or authority to implement any of their veiled threats.

For instance, I was told more than once that if I were to send in all the money owed, that I could save my credit despite being behind 90 and 120 days on the mortgage. The sad reality is that once you have gone even 30 days delinquent on your mortgage, this 30 day late is sent to all credit reporting bureaus and you officially have a negative mark on your credit. The mortgage company will tell you this to extract as much money out of you as possible. This is also exactly why people get frustrated with the lenders because most people who pay attention to their credit scores know exactly what types of things impact negatively on their credit. When the collections departments tell you a bold faced lie, you lose all confidence in their ability to be truthful with you.

I was also told by someone in the collections department that after only 60 days the mortgage would be foreclosed and we would "be out on the streets" two weeks after that. This may be the case in some states; however in Florida the process runs from 120 to 180 days from start to finish a foreclosure. If I had not been informed of this fact by a friend, I may have packed up and moved on way ahead of the legal time we had to vacate the home we were in. Since we wound up filing a bankruptcy, it became a mute point.

In the course of researching this book and other topics, I have spoken to various people who have gone through similar situations and one story that stands out was one from a young couple who after getting behind for 90 days or three payments. In their situation they were told by the collections department that if they were to send in any payment at all, that the collections department had the authority and could stop the foreclosure process. This is another bold faced lie. The collections department can only collect funds and nothing else. If the foreclosure action has begun, the only way to stop the action is to get an exact figure from the attorney handling the file and submitting the funds to them directly <u>in full</u> and getting the loan reinstated.

I am not sure if all the facts in the above example were true and what was said, but on the surface, there is no way that the collections department could have delivered what was promised. My last word of caution is that if something is promised by anyone in the collections department, get it in writing and ask them for their supervisors name so you can confirm the information is correct. Just take what is said and verify before you agree to send any money with the promise that something will be done on the other end.

✖ THE RULES OF THE GAME ✖

In many states there are different rules pertaining to what a collections department or collection company can do. There are guidelines that must be followed and some of those are not commonly known by the consumer.

For instance, the collections people cannot call you after 9:00 P.M. under any circumstances. There are penalties and fines that could be imposed if they were to break this provision. Remember this is not a state law, it is a federal law.

Another big mistake some mortgage companies make is to keep calling the borrower even after they have filed for protection under the bankruptcy laws. By law they are no longer able to hound you through the collections process. The protection under the bankruptcy laws also translates the same for credit card and other collection agencies.

All you need to do if any of these companies call you after you have filed a bankruptcy is to politely inform them that you have applied for protection under the federal bankruptcy laws and that they would need to speak to your bankruptcy attorney.

The action of filing the bankruptcy will certainly stop most of the phone calls, but the price you pay in future years in rebuilding your credit must be seriously considered before deciding to take that measure. There are some instances where a bankruptcy is really the only option. Just do not get railroaded into this option by a bankruptcy attorney who suggests you take this route. They care about one thing and that is the fees the bankruptcy will generate. One last thing to keep in mind, the person or entity that gets paid first in a bankruptcy proceeding is the attorney. Wow, imagine that?

The last word in this section is that you should play fair with the bank or mortgage company. If you make a promise to work with them and agree to send some money on a date certain and you don't send them the money, you will be treated as a liar and not given any credibility in future dealings. I have a simple credo that I live by in my personal and business life and that is:

Keep all the promises you make and don't make any promises you don't intend to keep. My word is my bond, my credibility and integrity are all that matter to me. I have walked away from real estate deals where I thought the person we were buying the house from was less than 100% coherent or not of sound mind. I never have to try and remember if what I said was the truth or do I have to remember if what I told one person is the same as the next, my story stays the same no matter what.

❦ FINAL THOUGHTS ❦

There is no doubt that going through this period in the foreclosure process was very stressful. The constant calls from the collections departments of the mortgage company and the slew of credit card companies we were in debt to was difficult because I was the one taking them. Since my wife is deaf, I could not pawn the calls off for her to take. The tone of the conversation ranged from pleasantly cordial to rude and combative.

You must hold your ground and not be intimidated by the gorillas on the other end of the phone and try as best you can to keep the lines of communication open at all times, especially if you are working hard to bring the payments current and save your house. Always remember to deal honestly and fairly with the mortgage company and don't do what I did and shut them out if you have a bad experience with one of the collectors who treat you badly.

My stubborn approach shut me off from the possibilities that may have been available to us to save the house, but I am a thick Frenchman and I definitely had a huge chip on my shoulder. If your intent is to save your home from the foreclosure, you owe it to yourself to swallow some pride and put up with these people, just don't be bullied. Do not be afraid to go over their heads and if you get the supervisor of a person, who has been abusive, report them. Remember to record whom you spoke to and what day and time the conversations took place.

One measure I have taken at times when I knew that the person I was about to speak to would give me a hard time was to inform them that since they always say that they are recording the call for "training" purposes, I would be recording the call as well. Sometimes I would get a very surprised person on the other end and other times, it was no big deal. I did find that there was less confrontation when they knew I was in fact recording our conversation.

In the next chapter we will be explaining the role and function of the Loss Mitigation/Workout Departments of the various banks and mortgage companies. Within this department will be the people who not only have the authority to make deals regarding repayment, but can also help you sell your house if you are way over financed and really have no other way out. I will explain how this department was forced to be created by the Federal Government and what can be accomplished with just a little work on your part.

So, you have taken a couple of punches from the collections department, you may have a little blood on your lip, but you are still standing and now you are ready to learn what the Loss Mitigation department can and must do for you. Get ready to speak to people who really can help. Too bad the loan is now over 90 days past due. Anyway, let's move on and learn about saving our homes from foreclosure or getting out from under all this debt.

Chapter 5

The Loss Mitigation / Workout Department

There was nothing more frustrating for me then when I found out that after having a foreclosure filed on my wife and I, dealing with the goons in the collections department and ultimately caving in and filing for bankruptcy that there may have been a way out of our financial dilemma. Knowing now that there may have been a way to save our house angers me to some extent, but it also motivates me to pass this important information along.

The way out of our financial mess was partially through the people in the Loss Mitigation (LM) or Workout department of the mortgage company we were dealing with. I guess it would have been nice if they told us we had an option. In fairness to the mortgage company, I think our decision to work through the bankruptcy kind of killed any chance we may have had at the time to construct a solution through the LM department. Although the Loss Mitigations will work with properties tied up in a bankruptcy, it usually takes the approval of the court as well as the Loss Mitigation department to get the deal done.

Some creditors may object to selling a property with what is perceived to be paper "equity" at a huge discount in order to get the debt and property out of the bankruptcy. The bottom line is that it is both the bankruptcy Judge and the person in the Loss Mitigation department making the decision.

The information contained in this section will detail the function, policy, and procedures that are part and parcel of the LM department. It may be helpful to know why this department exists in the bank or mortgage company at all since up until the early 1990's they simply did not exist in the capacity and importance they are today.

And today especially they are critical in aiding the workout process to avoid full blown foreclosures. That's the good news; the bad news is that they are literally overwhelmed by the volume and weight of the foreclosure tsunami sweeping across all four corners of our country.

❧ WHY THE LOSS MITIGATION DEPARTMENT ❧

If you were around or have any recollection of the late 1980's and early 1990's there was a banking/savings and loan problem in the United States. There were many small Savings & Loan companies in serious trouble due to originating bad loans on properties they had no business lending money on. Many of the loans were on speculative real estate deals where money was lent on the projections of great future gain from development and appreciation of the real estate. Doesn't this sound very familiar? Kind of like the speculative investors around the country trying to make a quick dollar speculating on the rapid appreciation rates.

Even former President Clinton and his wife were involved in a similar deal; it was just a widespread practice that led to the Federal Government forming yet another agency called the Resolution Trust Corporation (RTC). Their sole purpose was to assist the banks and mortgage companies liquidate their troubled loans and get rid of the properties the banks took back and in most cases were just handed back without the formal foreclosure process.

There were literally hundreds of millions of dollars worth of commercial, industrial, retail, vacant land, and single family properties sold to the general public for pennies on the dollar just to get them off the books and the RTC was in charge of getting rid of them all via sales through licensed real estate brokers and via general public auctions. It was a mess that the taxpayers of this country had to pay for. Now there's a big surprise isn't it?

Since most of these bad loans were backed by the federal government, the RTC had to assist in the disposition. They were also forced to take over insolvent Savings & Loan companies that were going under since most deposits are guaranteed by the Federal Deposit Insurance Corporation.

The Loss Mitigation / Workout Department

The Federal Government having learned their lesson from the RTC fiasco instructed; no make that mandated that any mortgage company or financing institution lending money that is backed by the federal government form a department that would mitigate or intercept these potentially bad loans so they would not get stuck footing the bill once again and have a flood of foreclosures on their hands again.

The government instructed the banks and mortgage companies to form the LM departments in an effort to work with the borrower (you & I) to take the non-performing loan and turn it around and make it a performing loan for the bank again. When I first heard this, my reaction was so what, they will just go through the motions and foreclose anyway and just write off the losses. Some certainly act this way at times, but the real compelling reason I believe the banks and mortgage companies have made a sincere effort to work with the homeowners are as follows.

The federal government also instructed the banks and mortgage companies that if they were to lend federally backed money, they would be penalized if a mortgage came back to them via a foreclosure. The banks were told that for every dollar of defaulted loans you have on the books, they were to set aside eight (8) times that amount in reserves for bad debt. This information was obtained through research and is deemed to be accurate and correct.

Think about this for just one minute; if the bank forecloses on a property with a loan balance of $100,000, they are forced to set aside $800,000 in a bad debt reserve. Last time I looked, banks don't make money unless they are loaning out money, thus the motivation for them to work with the homeowner to find an amicable solution.

❧ WHAT THIS MEANS FOR YOU ❧

Simply put; this means that you have an option besides foreclosure. My problem with this arrangement is that it would have been much better to get involved with the people in the LM department much earlier in the process. Lately, we are seeing a trend to get these people involved much earlier in the process, but simply not enough lenders are proactive enough as far as I am concerned. It seemed that in the past when your loan went into default your file was duplicated and a copy was given to the Foreclosure Department and one was given to the Loss Mitigation department and whoever got to the finish line first would prevail.

There were instances early on when we were working with homeowners where this certainly seemed to be the case. We were speaking to people from both departments and it seemed like they were pulling in opposite directions. In reality they actually were when you come right down to it. You should also note that every bank and mortgage company has different policy and procedures and no two are alike. Some have a great reputation of working with homeowners to arrive at a solution and others are just very difficult to deal with.

Not too long ago when the LM department got involved what happened is that your file was then assigned to just one person to work on. Now, every file is loaded on a computer with all the documents you may provide as well as a history of every conversation of everyone who has ever called on that mortgage account number. This is not bad in some instances as anyone you call can see where your file stands at any given time, the bad news is you lose that personal contact and the ability to build rapport with someone. I used to like the old way because after a certain point in the process I was able to get a real name and direct phone number of the person who actual had a file in front of them. You still should be able to get the individuals direct phone line or extension if they are serious about working a Short Sale, you just may not speak to that same person all the time. If you can't get that, they will at least give you a direct number to the LM department. Although these people have mountains of files they work with every day, they will make an effort to work with you if you are sincere in your desire to keep your property from being foreclosed. Also know that it is a numbers game for them and they will always work on the files that have the greatest chance of being worked out to a resolution that is favorable for the lender.

While speaking about files, I always take an informal survey while trying to build rapport with anyone in the LM department. As part of my conversation, I always ask how many files they are currently working for the bank or mortgage company. When these people were actually handling every file, the lowest amount of files any one person had at one time was 65, and the highest amount of files one person was handling was a whopping 225 and this was a few years ago. My guess is that those numbers have probably doubled at this time. I don't know how this guy did it and no one else has ever come close. I just assumed he was telling me the truth; he had no reason to lie.

There is a very good reason I bring this up, you never want to waste the time of these people or your file will be rotated to the bottom of the pile. This is a bad thing to happen since you want the representative in the LM department to be working with you on an option for you to save your house not burying the file in the "hopeless" stack. These people are in general trying to help you, help them by making their job easier. I will get into more detail later when submitting information and corresponding with the LM representative.

No matter what you are told by these people, always keep in mind who they are working for. I have witnessed first hand that I have been asked questions about the clients I represent that if answered would have weakened my case and only give them additional information that was really not needed for them to either approve or decline our request for a Short Sale. That is why I tell you to remember always that the LM representative may seem helpful at times, but they are getting their paycheck from the lender trying to foreclose your mortgage.

❧ WHAT ARE YOUR OPTIONS? ❧

Once your file has been sent to the LM department you will be contacted by them in an effort to work out a possible solution to save the house from foreclosure. The only three options you will have in most situations is a Mortgage Modification, Forbearance, or a Short Sale/Short Payoff.

Part of the process is for you the homeowner to supply current financial information in the form of a personal financial statement, current pay stubs, bank statements, sometimes tax returns, and the reason why you have fallen behind explained in the form of a "hardship letter". Some banks may require more or less information, but this is generally the basic information the representative in the LM department will need to determine what the best route to take are. They also want to make sure that your "hardship" is real and that your finances can not support the property in foreclosure.

❧ FORBEARANCE AGREEMENTS ❧

In no particular order of preference, the LM representative will first ask if you can begin making some sort of payment and if so, they will figure what you could pay if you were to sign on to a Forbearance Agreement. This agreement simply takes the amounts in arrears and is divided by the number of months you Forbearance Agreement is for and this amount is added to your regular monthly payment amount. For instance, say you were $3,600 behind in your payments and you were able to qualify to work a Forbearance Agreement your repayment plan may look like this:

Regular Monthly Payment:	$ 800.00
Back Payments:	$ 150.00
($3,600/24 Months)	
	———
New Monthly Payment:	$ 950.00

Once the 24 months have passed and you have satisfied the Forbearance Agreement, your payment reverts back to the original amount of $ 800.00 per month. It is important to note that this is the most popular and most frequently used tool by the LM department to get borrowers back on track. If your financial problems were only temporary and your income will support it, they should attempt to work this agreement every time. You may want to try this route but get turned down by the representative in the LM department if he or she feels that your current income would not cover the added monthly debt burden. My suggestion to anyone faced with that news from the LM department and they desperately want to keep the house is get a second or third part time job to make up that extra amount they are requiring. I know that is easy for me to say, but remember it is only a temporary situation.

The representatives in the LM department love to see a sincere effort and desire to save your property from foreclosure. I can say this because they run across so many homeowners who frankly do not give a crap about the house or working out a solution to their financial problems nor have any interest in taking responsibility for their own financial circumstances.

The Forbearance Agreement is signed by both you the borrower and the representative from the LM department. If you are interested in seeing what this agreement and a sample of the financial information you will be required to submit, please e-mail me your name and address and I will send out a copy in the mail. The e-mail address to request this information is crgcrest@msn.com. I was also able to locate a sample agreement online that will give you a general feel of what is contained in a standard agreement. Here is a URL that you can type into your computer:

http://www.ahfc.state.ak.us/Department_Files/Mortgage/RoboForms/SER/ser89.pdf

Here is another example that is longer and has more provisions:

http://www.docstoc.com/docs/590416/Home-Solutions-of-America-Forbearance-Agreement

❧ MORTGAGE MODIFICATIONS ❧

In the many years and numerous files I have worked on and assisted homeowners with I have only seen a small handful of Mortgage Modifications worked out between the mortgage holder and the borrower. That was up until the latest wave of foreclosures. Things are always changing with the foreclosure process; it is one of the reasons why I decided to update this book. I think one of the primary reasons for this fact is that so many mortgage companies who work these foreclosures are simply overwhelmed by the volume of foreclosure filings coming their way. When there is a loan servicing company merely servicing the loans for a third party, the loan modification is much more difficult and time consuming since the servicing companies have no real authority to make changes to the mortgage in any way.

In the simplest terms, a Mortgage Modification is simply an agreement between the lender and borrower to materially change the terms and conditions of the original mortgage signed when the loan was originated. Obviously there are numerous forms that need to be produced, signed, and then recorded on public record.

In most Mortgage Modifications I have seen the changes made were in the interest rate or the payment schedule. There are other forms of Mortgage Modifications where the amounts that are in arrears are added to the back of the loan and the other terms and conditions of the loan remain intact. In other words, if a borrower is behind on payments in the amount of $5,000 and their current principal balance is $250,000 the mortgage company simply adds that $5,000 to the back of the $250,000 as a sort of additional payment or balloon amount due when either the property is sold or refinanced. This too is recorded in public record and signed by all parties.

I always ask for this agreement especially if the homeowner I represent has had a temporary financial setback, is currently making enough to make the regular monthly payment but does not have anything saved to make up the big amount that is in arrears. Again, this all depends if the bank or mortgage company servicing the loan has the authority to make this sort of agreement and get it approved in a hurry.

You can again log on to the internet and view a simple Loan Modification Agreement at these two URL's:

http://www.lawca.com/useful/files/F02901.rtf

http://www.docstoc.com/docs/827459/Mortgage-Modification-and-Extension-Agreement

❧ SHORT SALE / SHORT PAYOFFS ❧

The Short Sale / Short Payoff allows for the homeowner to get out from under the mortgage debt without having a full-blown foreclosure on their credit record. Short Sales are usually allowed when a property is over burdened with debt. I could get on my soapbox and blame the mortgage companies for offering loans at as much as 125% of value, but I won't since we are teaching not preaching here in this discussion. Besides, the subject has already been brought up already.

Similar to the Forbearance Agreement and Mortgage Modification, you will be asked by the representative in the LM department to supply documentation in order for them to consider a Short Sale payoff. Your financial situation must clearly paint the picture that you will not be able to bring the loan current or be able to make payments in the future. Your "hardship letter" will also need to have a good reason why you got into such deep trouble to begin with. If the numbers make sense to the mortgage company, they will allow a Short Sale if the paperwork and contract is submitted in a timely and complete manner.

A Short Sale is simply the mortgage company agreeing to in most cases taking a discount on the amount owed to them on the loan in order for the homeowner to sell the property to either an end user or investor. There are complicated ratios that banks use to determine what the minimum they will take for any transaction and the amount they will discount the loan, but for the purposes of this book, we will not get into them. Just know that those ratios or percentages are based on what value the property is appraised at when the Brokers Price Opinion (BPO) is completed on the property.

To accomplish the Short Sale, you must realize that it is very much time sensitive. In some states where the time line for the foreclosure sale is very short, you really need to have all your information complete and in proper order right away if you have any hope of getting your Short Sale request accepted. Keep in mind that the legal action of the foreclosure continues along at a good pace regardless of what you are doing while the Short Sale package is being assembled and sent to the LM department. I know that the process has slowed considerably over the past year of the Short Sales I have worked on. Again, the amounts of defaulted mortgages being processed by the LM departments are at an all time high right now.

The good news is that if your offer makes sense and the representative in the LM department gets an approval to accept the Short Sale payoff, they have the ability and authority to delay the foreclosure sale in order to close the deal you have with your buyer. The bad news is that regardless of when or if it is sold, you the seller will get a big fat ZERO dollars at closing. The banks and mortgage companies will not allow you to walk away with a dime if they are forced to discount the loan in order for you to sell the property. It's kind of common sense, why would they allow you to walk away with anything if they are taking a loss on the payoff?

The Short Sale will also be contingent on you having the ability to negotiate any junior liens like second mortgages or judgments of any kind on the property. The first mortgage holder doesn't care about any second mortgage holder and will most times limit what they can receive to just $1,000, regardless of how big the second mortgage is. Their feeling is that if they have to discount their loan to make the deal happen, the junior lien holders will take whatever they will give them and be happy. Most times the second mortgage holders will take something, but I can assure you they are never happy about it.

I have personally handled negotiations for numerous Short Sale deals and I should warn you if you try and do this on your own, you must pay attention to details and always know when critical dates in the foreclosure are approaching. If you know someone who understands this process and can get them involved early enough in the process, they can and will handle all the negotiations for you while finding a buyer for the home as well. For this reason, we are beginning to get Accountants and financial professionals involved. I think that they are uniquely qualified to handle the paper work and understand time lines and the importance of submitting information completely and accurately.

This is a critical part of my current business as we work daily on Short Sales and the more we do the more successful we are in obtaining a positive solution. I wish I could say we were 100% successful, but that would not be true. Occasionally, we will run into a representative in the LM department that is just hell bent on not working out a deal no matter how compelling a case we make. Sometimes our assumptions of value are off and sometimes their assumptions are wrong and we have to just lick our wounds and move on.

There are no guarantees that you will be successful, but you owe it to yourself to at least give it a try. It is always better to have some negative bumps on your credit that may show late payments or 90 to 120 days past due as opposed to having a full blown foreclosure on the report. I speak from experience regarding this issue as I paid the price with severely damaged credit for many years after our foreclosure.

❧ REASONS WHY THE LM DEPTARTMENT WILL WORK WITH YOU ❧

One of the primary reasons the LM will work with you to resolve the problem was mentioned earlier, that being the restrictions the Federal Government will place on future lending. The second equally important reason is that banks and mortgage companies are not in the business of owning and maintaining properties. Quite frankly, they do a lousy job.

You should know that although they have a vested interest in working the loan out of trouble. In many instances, the bank or mortgage company may be servicing the loan for an investment group. These investment groups buy large pools of mortgages and hire companies to service the loans, they are basically paid a fee to collect the payments, make sure the escrow impounds are made, make the insurance and real estate tax payments from the escrow account, issue the year end tax information and whatever else falls under their management agreement.

It may serve to reason that if these servicing companies end up losing too many accounts to the foreclosure auction, their revenue from servicing these accounts go down and it may lead to the investment group taking their portfolio of mortgages to another company for servicing. Also know that the servicing companies are impotent to do anything as far as any direct negotiating with you the borrower. They receive their marching orders from the owners of the pool of mortgages they are servicing and no one else.

The important point to know here is that sometimes the representative in the LM department will need to run the forbearance agreements and Short Sale requests by the investors they service the loan for in order to get an approval. This has been the case on numerous loans I have worked on personally and usually takes a little more time to get done. It has always taken much more time to complete a Short Sale request when we are working on a loan that is being serviced by a third party as opposed to dealing directly with the lender who is foreclosing.

One of the first questions I ask when I finally do talk to a live person representing the lender is whether the loan we are working on is owned by that lender. If I am told that they are simply servicing the loan, I will make sure everyone that works on that file knows that. It does make a difference on how quickly correspondence gets turned around.

The main and most important reason the LM representative will work hard to get the deal done with you is that if the numbers make sense to them. On the representative's end of things, the deal will fly if from the LM department standards and formulas they use to determine if they should work with the homeowner, they will "net" enough after all closing costs.

Finally, another very important reason they will work with you is that you have done everything they have asked you to do in submitting the financial information and other documentation they need to process your request. You have been honest and straightforward with them and the rapport you may have developed over the weeks if not months have had an impact in the effort they have expended to produce a positive outcome.

There is nothing like working out an agreement for a homeowner who realizes they are going to get to stay in their home if they just follow through and work the repayment plan that has been negotiated out. I also get the same satisfaction when a homeowner who was straining under the weight of being over-financed is able to walk away and have their house sold without having a foreclosure on their credit record.

REASONS WHY THE LM DEPARTMENT WILL <u>NOT</u> WORK WITH YOU

In the experience that I have had in direct negotiations with loss mitigation representatives that would not work with me, I have found that the biggest reason deals don't get made is that the clock simply runs out and there is no time to iron out an agreement. As I have mentioned already, the timelines keep getting dragged out further and further as these lenders are forced to handle more and more foreclosure cases. There are only so many hours in the day and they simply can only work so many files at one time.

This is the main reason why it is so important to start the negotiation process as soon as possible so to give yourself a fighting chance in saving your house. Since the entire process takes weeks to complete and the people reviewing your file are swamped with other files to work on, they must have a compelling reason to find your file, run the numbers, get an approval, and eventually agree to a deal.

Even if you do all you are supposed to do, sometimes the numbers will simply not make sense to the LM representative and they will not agree to work with you to come to a mutual agreement. If after you have submitted all your information and your income will still not support the new payment amount, there is no need for them to keep the file open. They will not grant you forbearance in January if they know come February you will not be able to make the payment. It is strictly a numbers game at that point.

By far the quickest way to get a LM representative to bury your file is to cop an attitude with him or her and demand attention be paid to your account. This will simply not work and your file will not only be rotated to the bottom of the stack of files, it may never see the light of day again. Since they have gone to basically a paperless system where all data is loaded on to a computer, I'm sure they file problem files and code them differently than loans that they feel have a chance of being worked out.

The people in the LM department always work on the files that have the greatest chance of producing a positive outcome for them. They are the tollbooth operators and they control the flow of traffic, they cannot or will not be rushed. No amount of calls, faxes, e-mails, or messages left on their voice mail will make a difference. As a matter of fact, it will create the opposite result.

Your deal and request for a work out will also die if you have lied or not submitted the entire package of documentation they have asked you to provide. Early on in my experience with the people in the LM department I would send bits and pieces of the Short Sale package and the deals were stalling big time.

I was finally told that if the package was not submitted in its' entirety, they would not even look at it. It sure would have been nice if someone told me that to begin with.

Finally, the last reason they may not work with you is that they will be unable to get the deal approved by the investor who owns the mortgage. In some cases the property they are foreclosing on may have a much higher value than the delinquent mortgage balance. If this is the case, the investors will feel that they will not lose if they are forced to foreclose since they will get all their money back when the house is re-sold. Therefore, they will not agree to any deal since they are virtually guaranteed to get their money back.

✖ CLOSING THOUGHTS ✖

There is simply no substitute for taking clear decisive action as soon as you are falling behind on your mortgage. Communication is the key, no matter how unpleasant it may be at times. If you sincerely attempt to keep in contact with the mortgage company letting them know what is going on, you will be ahead of 99% of the rest of the crowd who do nothing and ignore the problem.

I would also suggest you find someone who has some experience in dealing with banks and mortgage companies who can walk you through the process of negotiating your debt. There are many "investors" out there that promise people the world, but never deliver on their promises. They are after one thing and one thing only, as much of your equity as possible.

I have also observed in my travels that sometimes the hardest part of this ordeal for the homeowner is coming to grips with the reality of the situation and simply making the decision to stick it out and make it work or pack it in and move on.

When the time came for my wife and me to decide, it finally boiled down to both our physical and mental health being much more important than any one house built of wood we had lived in for just a few years. It didn't kill us, it only made us stronger.

You should know now that you have options that you may have been unaware of before. Be proactive with your financial problems and work out a solution that is in your best interest. As I mentioned earlier, we have been working with banks and mortgage companies for more than just a few years as of this writing and we offer free, no obligation consultation services.

If you are interested in getting involved in a free e-course you can sign up at www.clydegoulet.com

Chapter 6

To Sell Or Not To Sell – That is The Question!

❧ IT COMES DOWN TO A PERSONAL DECISION. ❧

This is a question I am asked constantly by homeowners we are working with. Most people have trouble making every day decisions, so when a huge decision whether to keep the house, continue the fight, or just sell it and move on come up, there is a real reluctance to make that tough decision. There is something about making that decision that is so hard for people to come to grips with. The decision becomes an emotional roadblock.

I always tell homeowners to forget about the emotional attachments to the property and look at the dollars and cents picture. Usually there are memories that are associated with the house that people cannot separate from the financial issues they are dealing with. When I am asked to make such suggestions on such a decision, I will simply say that I have no authority or desire to be a part of such a personal decision.

In my situation, the house we lost to foreclosure was the first house we ever had built from the ground up. Granted it was built by a large track builder, but my wife and I still picked the design, the lot it was on, and the colors. There was a part of us in that house that was hard to let go. We watched that place rise up from the ground, took pictures of every step in the construction, and were proud to have friends and family over. We had holidays there, good time and bad time there as well. It was hard to finally let it go.

Your decision will be much the same. There will be things you have no problem forgetting about the place, and there will be things that you will take with you no matter when you decide to vacate the house. It is human nature and it is unavoidable.

With any decision of this importance, the facts and options must be clearly spelled out and to follow are the main questions and issues I ask and have answered by the homeowners I deal with. After this little game of twenty questions, the homeowners have usually come to some sort of decision one way or another.

Although I am always striving to see the homeowner stay in their home, sometimes the economics of the situation make it impossible for them to accomplish that goal. When all the questions have been answered and the financial numbers run, the reality of the situation determines what direction they will eventually take. Sometimes the reality is that they must try and save the home because they would not be able to afford any other location. Other times it is simply a very easy economic decision to make; the house they are thinking of saving is simply unaffordable for them.

❧ MAIN ISSUES/QUESTIONS TO CONSIDER: ❧

The first priority is determining what the homeowner can afford regarding their house/shelter payment. Clearly if the financial problems were only temporary and the homeowners are moving back to getting their feet on firm financial ground, then this issue may be a non issue. If the financial situation is one that will need many months to fully recover, then another strategy may be needed.

One of the most important payments we all make every month is for the roof over our heads. It would not matter to me if I had to put up with renting an apartment for a short period of time, knowing that the alternative to no shelter is sleeping and living out of my car. So, simply put, figure out what you can afford and make a decision based on that amount you have allocated to shelter.

If you have been able to work through a forbearance agreement with the mortgage company, chances are your monthly payment will increase to meet the repayment plan. Is your new payment amount going to strap you even more? I have seen many homeowners try the forbearance route, pay four to six months of the agreement and some little thing like a car repair bill happens and the house of cards falls in once again. Try and build in a cushion of some sort or set up a reserve for just this kind of situation that may come up when you least expect it.

The forbearance agreement has been a major benefit for many homeowners, enabling them to keep their homes while getting back on their feet. There is nothing wrong in giving it a try, even if you know things will be tight. You can always sell the property somewhere down the line if you have to. Bottom line is that you stay in control of your property, not the bank or mortgage company. We will get into a full-blown discussion of the Bankruptcy issue in Chapter 8.

The next question I ask the homeowner is if they had a budget before they got into the financial trouble? About 90% of the time I am told they did not have a budget or would not know how to set one up. The answer to this question always blows me away and it never surprises me either.

Before you think that I am looking down my nose at anyone who does not have a home budget, let me tell you a little secret. My wife and I did not have a budget either, and I have no excuse. You see my degree from college is in Accounting/Business Administration. What kind of idiot with a college degree in Accounting lets this happen to himself? It happens to Doctors, Lawyers, and pro athletes as well. I look back and it is kind of funny now, but at the time it seemed senseless to set up a budget since we had no money coming in anyway. It's a good excuse anyway.

Another question I ask and have the homeowner answer is if they could get by with downsizing the living space they currently have. It never occurs to people some time that they are living in too big of a house and that they could get by quite comfortably with a smaller house with smaller payments. I realize that simply switching houses is not like changing your socks; there is much work involved. But again, these changes do not have to be permanent unless you want them to be. If you find after some time has passed you need more space, you can always start looking for a bigger house or apartment.

Nothing worthwhile comes to you without a price being paid, this scenario is no exception. You may have to sacrifice a good neighborhood for just a marginal neighborhood in order to accomplish the switch. If you have some equity in your home, you may be forced via the IRS rules to purchase a house of equal size and price, it depends on your basis in the property and a tax accountant could tell you more on this subject.

If you were able, would you be willing to take on a second or third job to make the house payments? I hate asking this question, but if the income has not changed substantially for the members of the household, then this option becomes a very real possibility. I remember taking on some accounting work in the evenings for some small businesses in my home after we started getting back on our feet just to make ends meet and set some aside for an emergency.

I was lucky to have this skill to fall back on and was able to work out of my home and get paid, but I hated giving up my free time and being a slave to other people's deadlines for when the work needed to be done. Since I am a firm believer that no life experience is wasted, if I had not done that accounting work and hated it so much, I might still be counting beans somewhere instead of helping people like you through the foreclosure maze.

The last question is usually one that revolves around if the homeowner just needs to sell the house outright for other reasons. If the homeowners are separating, or a sickness will make it impossible for them to keep the house, or there is an upcoming relocation or job loss, then I will either make them an offer on the spot that is fair and equitable or I will give them some information regarding what to look for in a Realtor. Since I will discuss this later in the chapter, we will pass on my description of what makes a good Realtor for now.

Sometimes homeowners just need a fresh, clean start and selling the home is the most logical thing to do. If the homeowners have equity in the property and they are going to sell it on their own, I will give them some sure fire tips on how to drive traffic to the house and sample ads on how to attract buyers like moths to a flame. Chapter 7 will give you the condensed version of what has become a home study course I have developed. Every Realtor should buy it; if they did their incomes would triple. As a matter of fact, most of the testimonials I have gotten at the website where I sell the course is from Realtors. You can check it out yourself at www.getyourfsbosold.com

If you do decide to sell the property on your own, I suggest you use the services of a Title Company or a real estate attorney who can walk you through the closing process while protecting your interest. Selling a house on your own is not as hard as it may seem, but it will take some time and attention to detail. Besides, who knows your house better than you do?

❧ PEOPLE WHO WILL TRY & INFLUENCE YOU DECISION ❧

Investors will come a knocking, especially if you have equity in the property and they think you may be in desperate straights. In my area of the country in Central Florida, most homeowners who are working through a foreclosure will get reams of mail from all sorts of people claiming they are trying to "help" the homeowner when in reality they are trying to separate you from your house and take whatever equity you may have at the same time. I said most, not all will do this. Just protect yourself at all times.

You will also be contacted by investors via telephone and even in person. In all the years I have been actively working in real estate and investing I have never been so bold as to go knock on someone's door asking about their house. Number one is that I think it is downright rude, and second I wouldn't want to be knocking on someone's door after they just had a bad phone conversation with someone from the lenders collections department. I like my teeth where they are!

The people calling you will be asking you about your intentions with the house and whether you would be willing to sell the house for what is owed on it. Others will attempt to negotiate down the amount of your equity they will pay you to buy the house. I understand the thinking of the investor and their desire to make some money on any property they go through the trouble of buying, however I would never take advantage of another person's difficult situation for my own gain.

I have had a few instances when I could have taken advantage of a situation where a homeowner did not know the true value of their house and was willing to sell it to me for way below market value. Come to find out the elderly man I was negotiating with was starting to have the early symptoms of senility. I contacted his daughter who lived in the next town over and instructed her that she needed to get involved and not let him give his house away since it was the only real asset he had in his life.

Don't worry about me, I got two referrals from that mans daughter that made me twice what I would have made on her fathers house. I never take

79

advantage of people and you should be on the lookout for those who prey on the uneducated and vulnerable. The bottom line in dealing with any investor is to know whom you are dealing with.

The other points I would make when dealing with investors is to really look at the offer they are giving you. Is the offer really fair to you? If it seems more one sided in favor of the investor, ask why and get a good answer. If they have agreed to make up back payments and have assumed some risk, then they are entitled to ask for a little more since they are bailing you out and saving your credit.

I would also check if the deal is a win/win deal for both. Much like the point above, there has to be some give and take in every deal, but the deal where both parties feel as if they got a good deal is the one you should be after. I am also realistic and understand that some property owners are literally backed into a corner and must make the deal even if it is a bad deal on paper. There is such a thing as cutting your losses and moving on. This is a decision only the property owners can make.

A final word on investors; if you have been promised anything from anyone looking to buy your house, make sure it is in writing. It is amazing how selective memory can pop up and hit the buyer just when they are supposed to do something they had verbally agreed to do. It is not that I don't trust people to do what they say they are going to do, I just want it in writing signed by both parties so there is absolutely no question as to who was supposed to do what and when.

It is well worth the time and effort to get the terms and conditions of your real estate deal in black and white in the form of a contract signed by all parties. There are no guarantees that nothing will go wrong or the buyer will not follow through, however my experience tells me that those types of problems are less frequent when the contract clearly spells out chapter and verse what everyone's responsibilities are as it pertains to the contract.

Also have the contract checked by either a real estate Attorney of someone at the Title Company to make sure every "T" is crossed and every "I" dotted. I would always suggest as well that anyone purchasing a property from me put some money up down on the property and it be held by the party that will close your deal. One final thought on your contract; I would also make that deposit non-refundable if the Buyer has gone through the inspection period and when time comes to close the deal, they change their mind and back out. Again, just watch out for your best interest.

❧ DEALING WITH REALTORS ❧

Before I get into this discussion, I must admit that I have a passionate dislike for many Realtors in general. Most of the bad ones give the few good ones a bad name. The main reason for my dislike for them is that many times when we are selling an investment property we have taken over from a distressed seller, we are educating the Realtors as to market value and some of the questions we get are just plain stupid. Most have no business sense and do not understand what we do and how we help people in foreclosure to get rid of their houses.

Generally, the first question out of their mouths is how much of a commission are we paying. The main reason for my dislike is that in order for a residential real estate broker to sell your house they must price it low enough to bring buyers into the market that will qualify to buy your house. Since their job is to represent you, they should be working on getting the highest price possible; not looking to discount the house to a point where more people can buy your house.

They also fail to realize that if they took the time to know what we have discovered while working with banks and mortgage companies in the negotiating of debt; that they could help a homeowner who comes to them to list their house even if they are overleveraged. The Realtor should learn how they could still earn a real estate commission if they just understood that if they helped the homeowner negotiate off some of the debt, it would build enough of a cushion into the deal where they could get paid.

My other challenge is with the local area board of realtors here in the Orlando area. I have contacted them maybe a dozen times offering to teach classes to realtors about how to properly work Short Sales. Since Short Sales are my area of expertise, I figured they would jump at the chance of educating their members. Forget it; they care about one thing and one thing only; collecting the membership dues from the Realtors. It's a sad pathetic commentary to the state of affairs at this bureaucracy that while the Realtors they pretend to represent are having trouble making a living and they do nothing to assist them during these rough times.

Enough with the trashing of the Realtor profession, the good ones are very good and the bad ones are very bad. I would certainly get as many testimonials or names and numbers of past clients they have helped sell their houses for. Interview them like you would interview anyone about to work on your behalf. If they are good at their job, they will be able to furnish you with many names and numbers of people who have been satisfied with their work and efforts on their behalf. A testimonial from a satisfied customer is one of the most powerful marketing tools around.

Once you feel comfortable that the agent knows what he or she is doing, find out if they are primarily a "listing" agent or a "selling" agent. There is a big difference when it comes to agents who simply go out and give the sales presentation to the homeowners to try and get them to sign the listing agreement and the ones who actually work in the trenches, bringing qualified buyers to the house and getting the deals closed. If I were using an agent, I would make darn sure they have been actively working with buyers and ask them if they are working with anyone at the current moment that may have an interest in your house.

You should also be aware that most items on the listing agreement are negotiable, including both the commission and the length of the listing agreement. Do not get sucked into long listing agreements. If they can't generate interest in three or four months, they won't generate interest in six or nine months either.

You will be told that the "going rate" for sales commissions in your area is a certain percent. You can save yourself literally thousands of dollars by simply asking for a lower commission rate. Simply tell them that you are willing to pay them x percentage based on a full price offer. If you accept an offer at less than the listing price, then you would expect them to adjust their commission rate down.

To Sell Or Not To Sell – That is The Question!

I would also ask them that if they sell the house without the help of another agent from a different office that the commission rate be discounted. They will tell you how expensive their marketing is and give you more songs and dances then you could ever see or hear on Broadway. Just remind them that there are dozens if not hundreds of real estate brokers out there and that you will shop around until you get what you want. The real estate sales world is extremely competitive; they will work with you, within reason.

As I mentioned very briefly above, another major point I will ask you to consider is the length of the listing agreement you will be signing. They will do everything in their power to get you to sign for as long as possible. Do not sign anything longer than three months; I don't care what they tell you about how long it takes to complete a transaction. Most deals can get done in less than three weeks from contract to closing if the buyer has been pre-approved and there are no major problems with the title on the property.

The longer the listing agreement, the more time they have to sit and wait for the phone to ring. The longer the listing agreement, the less pressure there is on the listing office to get it sold. Think about it, if they have a house and they tie it up with an "Exclusive Right to Sell" listing agreement that basically binds you to paying them regardless of who brings the buyer to the deal, they have no real incentive to get the house sold in any kind of hurry.

You can always renew for another three months if they are actively marketing the property and there is activity from other agents showing the house. Stick by your guns with these issues; they give you the power as the consumer and that is the way it should be.

Finally on this topic, you must keep the listing agents feet to the fire. Insist they provide you with an activity report detailing how many times the property was shown, where they are actively advertising and what the complaints are about the house that prospective buyers are being turned off by. Make sure they communicate with you, it is their job to do this and it is the most important part of the job of selling your house in my mind. If your agent does not give you the service you are paying for, go over their heads and talk to the Broker in charge.

If that does not work, file a complaint with the local or state real estate commission. Only do this if you have a legitimate gripe, you don't want people loosing their ability to make a living by jeopardizing their license status. If their actions warrant some disciplinary measures, then that would be handled through this type of complaint with the local and state real estate commissions.

In the current real estate market with so many properties continually being dumped on the market from banks and lenders, it is even more critical that your property be priced right. So many times we will see people make the mistake of not getting an unbiased appraisal done on their properties. I always get an appraiser to come out and give me a true estimate of value on any property I sell. Sure it cost me a few hundred dollars, but I know I will not be wasting time and marketing money advertising a property that is not in line with the market or competitively priced. Going through this exercise actually saves me money in the long run.

In closing this chapter, take a good hard look at the chapter to follow on selling the property on your own. I know that many people would rather utilize the services of a Realtor, but in reality, who knows your house better than you do?

There is serious money at stake when you are able to sell the house on your own. We are talking thousands of dollars, who at this point needs the money more, you or the Realtor?

Chapter 7

Selling Your House On Your Own

This section of the book may be worth thousands of dollars to you if you pay attention to some of the selling techniques we have used successfully for many years to sell houses at lightning speed. It is our business to work quickly and get houses sold when we are negotiating with banks and mortgage companies who give us a very narrow window of time to get the properties sold. We could certainly teach Realtors a thing or two and in fact we have.

This discussion will focus on what we have found to be the most critical aspects of selling any house when you consider establishing a selling price and how to handle the real buyer's and tire kickers who will call. The whole idea behind our system of selling houses resolves around making the process as convenient as possible for YOU the seller. Let's get started, get a highlighter or pen and pencil to take notes.

The very first thing we do, no matter how well we know a particular area or market is order an appraisal. The cost of a full appraisal runs about $200 to $350 depending on the size of the house and the market you are in. You should tell the appraiser you are looking for a true estimate of value, not what you think it might be worth. Too many people get caught up in the game where they compare what their neighbor Gladys two doors down got for her house two months ago and think they should get at least that much if not more since your house has better curtains.

You will never know if the neighbor had a superior house or a piece of junk and that is why it was sold for the amount it sold for. Your appraiser will also go outside your immediate area to pull comps if the trends in market price warrant a higher appraisal. The last thing you want to do is sell for less than the property is really worth or price it so high that no serious buyer will ever take the time to look at it. Getting an appraisal of the house in its' current condition will give you a starting point in estimating the houses current value and the potential future value after some needed repairs get completed.

If you were to complete some needed repairs or improvement while attempting to sell the house, you really should adjust the asking price up to account for these repairs. We have also found that most buyers will expect you to come off your asking price some as a function of the negotiation process. You can either choose to play or choose not to play the negotiating game. I tell the buyers we have an appraisal that is less than two months old and we are certain our asking price is right in line with what the true value is of the property. Simply put; I don't do a whole lot of negotiating. The price is what it is. This will turn some potential buyers off, but if both you and the buyer have done their homework then the price will be right on target.

Now that you have an idea what the house is really worth in the current market, it is time to begin to spruce up the appearance of the property. We will start with the interior of the property. The primary selling points of the house should be designed with the woman buyer in mind. Sorry guys, there is a mountain of evidence that the woman picks out what house the couple or family will live in. With that in mind you should focus your sprucing and fixing up in the kitchen and bathroom areas.

They both should be spotless and basically shine to the point of hurting your eyes. I know that you may have some budget issues when it comes to spending money on improvements on the house you are trying to sell, however our in-house statistics show that for every 1 dollar we spend in either the kitchen or bathroom, that dollar spent comes back between five to seven times. So for every $100 we spend in these areas, we routinely get $500 to $700 back in profit from the improvement.

After the kitchen and bathrooms are in tip-top condition, we go down a list like the one to follow and see if these items can be improved. If you have pets, people who don't have pets will be able to smell and tell the difference. If you have a smoker in the house, it will affect your ability to sell the house. We go through the following list on the interior of every house we sell.

- Carpets/Flooring

- Paint- Walls, Ceilings

- Change light fixtures if dated

- Change doors and or hardware if needed

- Clean interior windows

- New Blinds

- Patch holes in walls

- Service A/C – Heat Unit

- Have Plumbing Checked

- Change plug and switch plate covers

- Un-clutter closets/storage areas

- Throw out any old or unused furniture that does not belong

- Clean from top to bottom

After you have spent the time and energy to fix up the interior it is time to start focusing on the curb appeal. Your house should look as good as possible from the street as this will entice people to want to see how nice the interior looks. Start by looking at any old trees or shrubs that have grown out of control to the point that they diminish the look not enhance the look of your property. Does the house need a coat of paint? Are the trees that surround your house blocking the rooflines, hiding the overall look? Is the roof in good shape? How does the grass or sod look from the street? Do you have any old or junk cars in the driveway? Is the driveway messed up with oil leaks? You should not be surprised that even some minor flaws that you see will seem like big items to potential buyers.

These are the basics in getting the house ready from the outside. You should think about getting and planting some cheap flowers and replacing the mulch to freshen up the look. Remember to wash the exterior of the windows as well. Are there screens on all the windows and do they have holes or rips in them? One trick we have used very successfully in quickly improving the eye appeal of the property is installing a new front door. It cost between $300 and $500, but it really helps with that first impression.

The last tip on the interior and exterior is this. Ask someone who is naturally picky or fussy, like a mother-in-law (just kidding) to come over and give you an honest assessment of how the house looks and ask if there is anything that could be done to improve the look. I have also spent $100 for a home inspector to come in after we had done all our fixing up and have him give us a report on the condition of the house.

This money spent is not wasted since we can either use the good clean inspection report we just paid for as part of our marketing information or we will be alerted to something we may have missed in our revitalization of the property. In any case, it helps to have a different pair of eyes looking at the property before you start the full-blown marketing blitz. The sweaty work is done, now comes the mind games and the marketing that will drive people to the house.

To begin, you should sit down and create a one to two page flyer on the property. I prefer using a one-page flyer with the vital information on the front such as bedroom, baths, square feet, age of house, amenities such as pools, hot tubs, built in entertainment centers, garage, inside laundry room, or anything else that might be a selling point.

In areas where the school districts are superior, I will place the primary, middle, and high school information on the front of the flyer. In areas like Florida, the type of construction is important and I will put whether the house is block or frame construction. I would also put the lot dimensions if I have them as well. Always remember to put a phone number on the flyer that drives people to an answering machine. We will discus this more a little bit later.

On the back of the sheet, I have both a scaled down copy of the survey and the basic floor plan. If you can't find a real floor plan, use the basic floor plan from the appraisal you had done. You can also get the lot dimensions from the appraisal as well. You see, there is nothing wasted in my world of selling houses. You will see in a minute how the other money we have spent for inspections ties into this theme.

Now that you have your flyers produced, it is time to pick up a "For Sale By Owner" sign with one of those tubes you can put your information flyers in. While you are picking up this sign, pick up at least four directional signs with the words "House For Sale" and a big arrow pointing in one direction. You can get them at any Home Depot or Lowe's.

When you get the sign for the front yard, put your phone number in bold easy to read numbers on the sign driving them to your answering machine for additional information. Attach your info tube and stuff that sucker with your flyers. Never let the info tube run out of flyers. I always keep a count of how many have been taken from the tube not for any particular reason except to have an idea of how many flyers get snatched up before a buyer is located.

With the directional signs you have purchased it is now time to put them out on any major road that would lead directly to your house. You must be cautioned though; these signs will disappear very fast. Both the county and city municipal workers are instructed to pick these signs up and throw them away if they are placed on public property. In order to save a few bucks, we put them out either late Friday night or early Saturday morning and go pick them back up on Sunday night. This is a pain sometimes since not all the houses we market are right around the corner. You have to decide if it is worth burning up $10.00 to $20.00 worth of gas to save a $5.00 sign.

These directional signs should have the street address on them written in the main box below the arrow. I also put additional information like 3/2 indicating the house is a three bedroom two bath home. Or I will write 2,000 Sq. Ft. indicating the size of the house. It is up to you what you put along the edges, but the physical address must be in the main area.

We have done some statistical work on how our buyers have found our houses and more than fifty percent find our houses by driving around and being driven to the house by the directional signs. There are very few Realtors who use this strategy because it takes a little work. It is effective; do not overlook the importance of this tip. If you look at this method of driving traffic in just the dollars and cents realm of things, they are well worth the money and effort to put out.

The next step is placing a classified ad in the local newspaper. This ad again will drive people to your answering machine and the message we will get to in just a short time. We have tested if it is better to include the price in the ad versus not putting the price and we get just about as many calls either way. To follow are three formats that we use on a consistent basis because they work. They all hint of motivation to sell and do not give away too much information. You want the reader to be curious enough to call the number; that is your primary objective with the classified ad. No one has ever bought a house sight unseen just because they thought the newspaper ad was so great they didn't need to see the house to confirm their buying decision.

These are the three ads we use on a consistent basis:

**Lake Mary – MUST SELL, updated home in
appreciating area. 3/2 with 1800 sq. ft of
living space. Bring all offers. Call owner
123-456-7890**

**Lake Mary – OWNER RELOCATING SOON.
1800 Sq.Ft
3/2 newly updated, priced below value at
$ (insert price) No reasonable offer refused.
Call owner 123-456-7890**

**Lake Mary – WILL SELL TO BEST
REASONABLE OFFER BY
SUNDAY MARCH 10, 2008. Great 3/2
completely updated.
1,800 square feet, call owner at
123-456-7890**

These ads will drive calls to your phone and you don't want to be answering them yourself, it will drive you to a rubber room. Regardless of the amount of information we put in the ad such as bedrooms, baths and square feet in the house, there is always some idiot who's first question is "how many bedrooms and bathrooms does it have"? This is where you must take control of the selling process. Remember some wise words I was told once: Control is never given, it is surrendered.

Since you will be getting calls directed to an answering machine, you will get people who will not leave messages on a machine; that is just the way they are. It is a trade off, either talk to everyone in the world with a stupid question or speak to only the people who are truly interested in the property. You will also get many calls from agents who will try to get you to "list" your house with them for maximum exposure and the benefits of having a "professional" sell your house. Sometimes I want to puke when I hear this drivel. Who knows more about the positive aspects of your house than you do?

On the flip side, if your time is better spent working on other things and you feel that selling your house on your own is worth paying a real estate commission, then by all means let a Realtor list your house. I really don't mind mowing my own lawn, but I could be doing so many more things much more productive that will make me much more money than it cost me to have it done. Make sense?

The answering machine script I use in the sequence I give the information out is done for a reason, so try not to deviate from this too much. It is always better to have a female voice reading this message into the answering system; it just has a better selling effect. Here is the basic message we give out:

Hello and thank you for calling on the property located at 123 Main Street in Anytown. This home has been recently updated and has _____ Bedrooms and _____baths with _____Square feet under heat and air. We are asking $_____ And have based our price on a recent appraisal.

We invite you to drive by and pick up an information flyer from the front of the house that will highlight the other features of our home. We have also included a floor plan and copy of the survey on the back of the flyer for your convenience.

If you are traveling from the north, take lake street south, take a left on 1st street follow about 2 miles and after you reach the first stop sign take a left to 123 Main street.

If traveling from the south, take Lake Street north, right on 1st street and after you reach the first stop sign take a right to 123 Main Street.

If you are an agent calling, we may consider a co-broker commission, however the contract price would have to be adjusted to account for this. At this time we are not interested in listing the property.

If you have seen the exterior of the property and wish to view the interior, please leave your name, number, and best time to call and we will be in touch with you shortly. Thank you for calling.

It may seem like an awfully long message to you, but the reason we give the size and brief description along with the price in the first paragraph is that if the house is not in the prospects price range, they will cut out right away and not tie up your line listening to the rest of the message. It will also discourage the agents who will be calling and they may hang up right away.

The section with the directions to the property is crucial. I usually get on the computer and go to Yahoo Maps and pick a local busy intersection and get directions to the subject house from there. This will give you driving directions as well as approximate mileage from one point to the next. Check it out, we have used it and it is free.

The wording directed to the agents is designed to tell them that you may accept their offers for their clients, but they better build their commissions into their contract price. This will usually discourage them enough to not do much of anything. However if their clients have found the house and they are sold on it, the agent may have no choice. Remember, you are under no obligation to pay them a dime regardless if they bring you a contract or not. If they include a commission in their offer and you don't want to pay them, simply strike through that wording. Or, you can simply adjust their commission down to what you can live with. Remember, you are in charge and you call the shots.

When you have received some calls from people who have seen the exterior of the property and have an interest in seeing the interior it is time to call them back. Sit down at your convenience and return these calls with the goal being to get them all to come look at your house on the same day at the same approximate time. This usually blows people away. Why in the world would we want to get three or four parties looking at the house at the same time? The explanation is a little further down.

This next strategy we use plays on the psychological aspect of an article with a high demand, yet little quantity. In this case, you will be scheduling the showings of your house with the interested parties on a date that is convenient for you and a date when you get the most people in your home at the same time. Yes, that is right; you want all the prospects at the home walking through at the same time.

Once they are there, pass out to them the information you have on the house. If you have spent the money for a home inspection and it came back without major problems, then copy it and add that to your package. If you have a copy of the survey or a pest inspection report, give them that as well. If you have paid for an appraisal and the price you are asking is supported by the appraisal, then give them a copy of that too.

Think about the situation and visualize what is going on. There are maybe three to five parties who have shown enough interest to come see the house, all walking around thumbing through the vital information you have provided and all of them wondering if they might be losing the deal to anyone else who is walking through the house. We are all human; we all seem to desire most the things we can't have.

This scene will create a real sense of urgency with some of your prospects and may even lead to more than one offer being submitted on the property. We have and continue to use this approach for a couple of reason. One of the reasons is above; it is the circus atmosphere we try and create with the prospects that show up. The second reason is that our time is very valuable and we would rather have just one open house a week for the prospects instead of opening up the house every day for one party to waltz through and waste our time.

If the ground rules are set that you only show the property on say Saturday from 1:00 P.M. to 1:30 P.M., you are in control and you can concentrate on the house looking its best in that time period. Make no exceptions and your life will be easier and the process will seem much less stressful. We have also experimented with adding the showing times to the voice mail message and we have found we get just as many prospects either way.

Once you have found a willing buyer who is truly excited about the house and is ready to put their offer on paper, you can get a contract drafted by either an attorney or perhaps with the help of a realtor friend. If all else fails, pick up a contract at the office supply store, fill it in the best you can, and have the title company or attorney check it out and see if it is filled in properly. I would strongly suggest you use either a Title Company or a competent Real Estate Attorney to handle your contract and closing.

These contracts are not rocket science, however when people who are not used to dealing with real estate contracts begin to fill these out, they freeze and think they will lose their first born if they make a mistake on the contract. The four critical points that must be somewhere in the contract is as follows:

-Contract Price

-Closing Date

-Deadline For Financing Approval

-Earnest Money Deposit

You could also add a couple of more items to that list like personal property such as the stove, refrigerator and dishwasher to be included with the house or NOT included in the purchase price of the house.

The last piece of information before you sign the contract and get the wheels in motion would be to get from your buyer a "pre-approval" letter from their bank or mortgage company. You may want to make this point clear to anyone who makes an appointment to see your house. You want to be dealing with true prospects, not mere suspects who couldn't buy a doghouse, never mind your house. You have every right and duty to yourself to ask for this, it is not out of the realm of the real estate world.

As a matter of fact, on some of the higher priced homes we have sold this way, we have made the pre-approval letter a sort of "ticket to entry" into the house. When we returned the calls and told the potential buyer what time the house would be available for showing, we instructed them that unless we were handed a copy of their pre-approval letter at the door, they would not be able to view the property. We ticked off more than one party when we stuck by our guns and it was kind of fun. Other buyers were inside walking around and they were at the front door straining their necks to get a look inside. Again, we were in control of the selling process.

I would also be remiss in mentioning that if there is a serious, material defect with the property that is not visible with the naked eye; this situation must be disclosed to your buyer. In this day and age where no one takes responsibility, it is important that the transaction be fair and honest. Never try and purposely deceive a buyer if you know of a major problem with the house that will be discovered when the new buyers are in the house.

Although you may have offered the prospective buyer's inspection reports to review, you do have a duty to disclose any major defect that is not visible to the naked eye, regardless if the buyers spend their own money for a property inspection.

A final note about the transaction; once your buyer has met their financing contingency it is time for the closing agent to do their thing. In Florida we can either close with an attorney or a title company. We always choose to use the services of the title company. For one reason, they are usually cheaper and second are that they are a third party facilitator, they represent neither the buyer nor seller exclusively.

Their fees are derived from the title insurance they write for the seller that insures that they are passing clear and transferable title to the buyer. They are also paid by the buyer for title insurance that warrants that the title they are receiving from the sellers are clear from any and all encumbrances, liens, or judgments and that the title to the property will be transferable when they come to sell the property as well.

Their fees are generally pretty much standard with no one company charging much more or less then the next. They will handle all the recording of the documents on public record and will work hand in hand with the lender that is funding the deal for the buyer.

When you consider how much money just this short section may have saved you in real estate commissions, it is worth the low price of this book. If you have any doubt about the contract issues, use an attorney; it will be well worth the money you spend. If you would like to pick up the full blown home study course I have been selling online that has received rave reviews even from Realtors, just go to www.getyourfsbosold.com and check it out.

One final thought on this section of selling your home on your own. Clearly these tips and tactics will work better when there is a Sellers market as opposed to a Buyers market. But the bottom line again is that if your property is competitively priced, the techniques should and will work for any type of real estate cycle we may be in. The bottom line is that no one knows your house better than you do. You are infinitely more qualified to sell a Buyer on the benefits of buying your property over any other choice they may have in the market.

The next chapter deals with the Bankruptcy option and what may or may not be a viable option for your future. It will be a decision only you can decide. I will add my two cents anyway.

Before you move on, here are a few sample flyers I pulled out of a file for you:

CONGRATULATIONS!!

You Now Hold $50,000 in Your Hands

Lakefront High & Dry Lot With POOL

PRICED $50K BELOW 2006 APPRAISAL
(See Other Side!!)

$ 325,000.00

This property has two master suites under the spacious 2,370 square feet of living space. There are many custom features in this home that included a formal living & dining room that complements the split plan design. With a beautiful island kitchen with 48" white cabinets along with a state of the art computer nook off of the bedroom hallway ads to the modern look and design of this home. Built in 2002 and is one of the highest and driest lots in the subdivision. With three bedrooms and two and a half baths, this home is available immediately to the right family looking for a great house at a great price. Call the number below immediately if you would like to see the inside of this home.

* Security System	* Irrigation System	* Lakefront
* Central A/C System	* Pool With Heater	* Appreciating Area
* Schools Close By	* Waterfall	* Block Construction
* 2370 Heated Sq. Ft.	* Screen Enclosed Pool	* Two Car Garage

Clyde Goulet
Lake Mary Realty, Inc.
407-***-**** (Office)
407-***-**** (Cell)

Would you like your $50,000 in $100 or $50 Dollar Bills?

SEE OTHER SIDE FOR IMPORTANT INFORMATION>>>>>>

OWNER FINANCING or LEASE/OPTION

1616 Brady Drive, Deltona Florida

3 Bedroom 1½ Bath POOL HOME

$ 164,997.00 (OBO)

LOW DOWN PAYMENT, NO CREDIT CHECK!!

Seller to Pay Up To $4,000.00 Towards Closing Costs!!!

This property has been recently updated with fresh paint, refurbished Terrazzo floors, new Dishwasher & Disposal, new outside A/C unit all under 1,239 square feet of living space. There are many nice features in this older home that must be seen to be appreciated. Roof was replaced in 2003 and with a screen enclosed built in swimming pool for entertaining or simply your private retreat. Call the number below immediately if you would like to see the inside of this home.

* New Roof in 2003	* New Dishwasher	* Fresh Paint
* Central A/C System	* Pool With Enclosure	* Appreciating Area
* Schools Close By	* Near Highway	* Block Construction
* 1,239 Heated Sq. Ft.	* Fenced in Back Yard	* One Car Carport

Clyde Goulet
Lake Mary Realty, Inc.
407-***-**** (Office)
407-***-**** (Cell)

SEE OTHER SIDE FOR IMPORTANT INFORMATION>>>>>>

Selling Your House On Your Own

<u>NEW ROOF, NEW PAINT, NEW CARPET</u>

<u>ALL IT NEEDS IS A NEW OWNER!!!!</u>

<u>112 Ryan Court</u>

Oakland, Florida

$ 149,900.00

This property has just been painted inside and out and offers 1,632 square feet under heat and air conditioning. The roof has just been replaced and you still have time to choose your own carper color. There is new vinyl throughout the home that was built in 1988 and is of solid block construction. With three bedrooms and two baths, this home is available immediately. Call the number below immediately if you would like to see the inside of this home.

* All Appliances Stay	* Fenced in backyard	* Quiet street
* Central A/C System	* Close to Turnpike	* Stable Neighborhood
* Schools Close By	* Great Potential	* Block Construction
* 1632 Heated Sq. Ft.	* Motivated Seller	* One Car Garage

Clyde Goulet
Lake Mary Realty, Inc.
*407-***-**** (Office)*
*407-***-**** (Cell)*

*** See Other Side For More Important Information About This Great House***->>

Chapter 8

Bankruptcy – To File or Not To File: THAT is The Question!

✿ WHAT YOU NEED TO KNOW: ✿

There is seldom a less confusing time for most people when trying to make the decision to file or not to file for Bankruptcy (BK). Not only is it a hard decision to make, but they give us the option of what kind of BK to file as well.

When Mary and I filed ours, we quite honestly did very little homework, knew little if nothing about the credit ramifications; and thought it was the best thing to do for all parties concerned. We thought by filing the Chapter 13, we would be paying everyone back as the court had agreed, and then once the BK was over (after five years) we would come out smelling like a rose.

To credit bureaus and lender we came out smelling all right; but not like a rose. We came out smelling like a deadbeat and poor risk to the credit bureaus, no one would extend credit for us to buy a doghouse, never mind another house for us to live in.

Only you can decide what is best for your current situation. This chapter will attempt to shed some light on some of the issues we had going forward after the BK as well as my thoughts as to what I may have done differently knowing what I know now.

You should read this carefully, I am not an attorney, and I don't even play one on TV. You must seek and get sound legal counsel before any decision as critical as the filing of BK. It has become somewhat of an accepted practice in society these days to not take responsibility for bad decisions and just say screw the rest of the world and all these debts we have accumulated.

Please, I do not mean to dump on the people who sincerely need the protection the courts allow via the BK route. I am talking about the people whom make it a way of life to amass a huge mountain of debt by buying needless stuff, taking cash advances on credit cards, and then filing a BK and then doing it all over again in a few years.

If you doubt this is happening, when I was writing the original version of this book in the Spring of 2005, there is heavy pressure on Washington to change the BK laws to favor the banks and credit card companies who spend millions on lobbyist every year to change consumer lending laws. Well, they did just that since the first version of this book was printed and congress passed sweeping changes in the Bankruptcy laws that you should all be aware of. I will highlight those new changes as we move forward in this chapter.

WHAT KINDS OF BK ARE THERE?

<u>Chapter 13</u> – Is the most common as of right now. A Chapter 13 BK is basically a petition to the court to allow you to reorganize your debt and monthly payment to better pay back your creditors over time. The attorney we hired to walk us through this process, had us fill out some paperwork that detailed all our debt as well as all the income we had coming in to offset all the debt.

Once the individual creditors are listed and the attorney then petitions the court to accept the list of creditors as the ones you will pay back. Any other creditor who you may have forgotten or has unsecured debt against you will be allowed to petition the court to have their claim included into your BK petition.

There are two kinds of debt; secured and unsecured. The secured debt simply means that the creditor has extended financing on either a property or a vehicle and the property or vehicle was pledged as the collateral for that loan. Their "security" in the money that was lent to purchase the home or vehicle, is the physical asset of the home or vehicle.

The unsecured creditors are primarily the credit card companies. They lend you money based on your signature and credit standing, with no collateral to come after should you fail to pay off the debt. Department store charge cards also fall under this category, regardless if you have purchased home furnishings with them or not. Many furniture stores extend credit to people only to have them file BK, sell off the furniture and they are left holding the bag.

Once the court and the creditors have approved your BK petition, you are told what your new monthly payment would be. Let me share our experience with you; it really is kind of funny and will serve as a good lesson. For the purpose of highlighting the changes in the BK laws, here is what my BK filing was all about and how it came to be.

My wife and I were having trouble making our $863.00 per month mortgage payment on our primary residence. We were not even paying on the credit cards at that point and we had about 18 months left on our car payment as well. The attorney we used meets with us and says that the court has allowed us to file the Chapter 13 and maybe save our house. The good news was that our payment that we would make to the court trustee who would then distribute the payment to the creditors per the courts orders would be $1,416.00 per month.

Our new monthly payment was $1,416.00!! I'm sitting there thinking that this attorney knew that we were having trouble making the $863.00 per month payment, how in hell did he think we would be swinging the $1,416.00 per month? Then I remembered that the BK attorney gets paid first, he didn't give a rat's rear end if we sunk, and he would get paid anyway. I looked at my wife, smiled and signed off on the plan for a total of 60 months. Five freaking years!

We got through it, but not because we didn't bust our asses and sacrifice things we really needed some times. I worked at least two jobs for most of those five years and we even had to borrow $5,000 form my wife's uncle Mitch for a couple of months. We paid him back, got really good at clipping coupons, and ate a lot of hamburgers and hot dogs.

There is one main reason I think we got through this and I will get back on my soapbox in one of the last chapters and give you the full details of why we have been so blessed since our BK.

One positive reason for filing the Chapter 13 is that the interest clock stops and your debt balances are paid off based on no additional interest being accrued.

Many people with temporary financial setbacks have been assisted with a forced repayment plan via the court trustee who collects your payment and then re-distributes the court ordered amounts to each creditor according to the repayment plan.

<u>Chapter 7</u> – Is a liquidation of assets to pay creditors. This action takes much less time and you still need an attorney to help you facilitate this legal action.

Much like the Chapter 13, you are asked to list all you debt and the assets you may have to pay off those debts. Usually when a person is advised to file the Chapter 7, the attorney and creditors know that your home maybe over leveraged with first and second mortgages that would make it virtually impossible for the first and second mortgage holder to sell off your property and bring in enough money to satisfy all the debt on the property.

What the creditors will do is search for any other "hidden" assets you may have such as boats, vacation homes, joint bank accounts, anything of value that could be liquidated to generate cash to pay off the creditors. If you have done anything that looks shady like take huge cash advances on credit cards just prior to filing a Chapter 7 BK, they may want to know where that money went.

For people who use this provision of the BK code to their advantage, they are able to get out of a bad financial situation faster. They also get back on their feet without a monthly payment they may not be able to afford and be able to start rebuilding their credit much quicker. Knowing what we know now, this is the route we should have taken; it would have been a lot less stressful. I thought I was doing the right thing and paying everyone back what we owed the creditors.

Finally on the Chapter 7, if you have qualified and elected to work the Chapter 13 and fail to make payments as you have agreed, the courts will automatically convert your repayment plan of the Chapter 13 to a liquidation plan of the Chapter 7. You have no say in the matter and they move quickly to make this happen.

<u>Chapter 11</u> – Business reorganization. I know our discussion here is personal finances, but in business this option is available and is much like the Chapter 13 available for the individual. I have worked in companies that had gone through the Chapter 11 and the process is similar to the Chapter 13, but the attorneys charge a heck of a lot more assisting with the Chapter 11.

By far the most important aspect of filing any BK action is to know what is best for you. You must take some time to sincerely think what your future finances look like and what kind of stress you can endure. The greatest tool that the Bankruptcy laws provide is for the homeowner to have an opportunity to save their home. In my mind there is no greater compelling reason than that to go through the ordeal.

GOOD REASONS TO FILE CHAPTER 13

I may have mentioned some of the benefits above, however the reason noted here are reasons and questions I should have seen back when I went through this.

If I had fallen behind and wanted to stop the creditors from calling me everyday and I knew the income situation was only temporary, the Chapter 13 would have been a good idea. If you are bombarded by multiple calls from creditors and you get sick of handling them, the Chapter 13 will stop those calls. If you do get a call after the BK has been approved, the creditor is liable for a fine and penalties under the fair debt collections act.

Chapter 13 is also not a bad idea if you truly have the ability to repay all your creditors and you are certain the new monthly payment will not be an unbearable burden to carry for the length of the repayment plan. One of the best aspects for us was that the interest clock stopped accumulating on all those credit cards we were forced to use in order to survive. Since we were making only the minimum payments in order to keep afloat, not having the interest accrue as we made the 60 payments per our plan was important and a positive in our minds.

As mentioned earlier, the main positive reason for us filing the Chapter 13 BK was the ability for us to keep and stay living in our house. We had only been living there a couple of years and we really had no other place to go. It was one if not THE driving force behind me working like crazy and making every payment as we did. Looking back, it was just a house and we buy them all the time now as investments, but back then, it was important and we needed to keep that house.

❧ BAD REASONS TO FILE CHAPTER 13 ❧

If you have just one or a couple of creditors, I think you should try and tough it out without making the jump into BK. Jobs are free; you can get a second job anytime you want. Like I said before, I worked two jobs and nearly killed myself in the process, but we had a mountain of credit card debt. If I had just the mortgage payment to contend with, we could and would have made up those back payment amounts in less than a year and a half.

Heck, we might have worked with the people in the workout department or loss mitigation on structuring a forbearance agreement that would have made sense for us. I know this was probably not an option back then, but in this time in history it is available to most people and they simply flat don't know about it.

I would also suggest against filing the Chapter 13 BK if you are just planning to stall. I really think the energy you would use in keeping a charade going would be better spent getting your financial life in order for real. Many people use the courts protection under the BK laws to just stall and string things along.

Maybe they are buying time in order to line up a move to another living situation, or maybe they are just playing a game. Just keep in mind that we are all given the same amount of time every day. I try not to waste other people's time, and I hate it when someone wastes mine because I will never get that time back again. It is lost forever.

If you know deep down that you will never be able to make a repayment plan proposed by the court, let them know and convert to the liquidation and start new. There is a lot to be said to not beating dead horses. Looking back, I should have probably just filed the Chapter 7 and been done with it instead of going the route we took.

❦ GOOD REASONS TO FILE CHAPTER 7 ❦

One of the most obvious positive reasons for filing the Chapter 7 is that you are given a quick solution to the stress that comes along with being in debt. Going this route will stop most of the annoying phone calls right away. It is the financial fresh start that people need sometimes to get their act back together. The Chapter 7 route certainly serves its' purpose, but only you can decide if the price is too high.

I have been told by some people that from the day their BK was accepted to the time they reestablished their credit to the point of being able to get another charge card was a little as 6 months. Now, I am not sure what kind of credit card it was or if they had to secure the card with a deposit. It may have been sort of like a debit card, however they went right to work on repairing their credit and it took less than a year for them to be able to get themselves back on their feet. Chapter 9 will get into how best to restore and protect your credit.

This fact alone was the reason I regretted taking the route I took. On the other hand, I felt I should have paid back the money we owed and the Chapter 13 BK was the only way to do that.

❦ BAD REASONS TO FILE CHAPTER 7 ❦

The single biggest negative about this route is that you are forced to liquidate all your assets to pay your creditors. This means the very real possibility of having to sell your homestead and any other asset the court may deem to be valuable enough to sell and pay creditors with.

I have spoken to people who informed me that they were forced to sell off family possessions and heirlooms as a result of going the Chapter 7 route. I have no personal experience with the Chapter 7 and hope that I never do.

Another aspect that I was made aware of is that if during your listing of all the creditors you happen to forget one or two and they have not been notified, they may continue to harass you and call you about your unpaid debt. Sometimes simply telling them you are in or have just been through a Chapter 7 BK will be enough to get them to lighten up.

Other creditors will sell their unpaid accounts to collection companies who will threaten you with everything under the sun. You will be forced to either respond or ignore them.

The absolute worst reason for filing either the Chapter 7 or 13 is because an attorney told you to do it. Unless the attorney is your family member and is working your case for free, then you want to question an attorney whose advice is to file a BK.

Just keep one thing in mind when an attorney tells you the best route is a BK; the fact is that out of all your creditors you list who you have owed money to for so long, the first party that gets paid from the BK process is of course your attorney. It's amazing isn't it when all is said and done, the lawmakers in Washington D.C. have set up all the BK laws to insure their attorney friends get paid first.

HERE ARE THE RECENT CHANGES IN THE BANKRUPTCY LAWS

This information was obtained from the NOLO Website at: www.nolo.com

The New Bankruptcy Law

The new bankruptcy law may make it harder to file Chapter 7 bankruptcy.

The latest changes to bankruptcy law may be making it harder for some people to file bankruptcy. And a few filers with higher incomes are no longer allowed to use Chapter 7 bankruptcy, but will instead have to repay at least some of their debt under Chapter 13. All debtors now have to get credit counseling before they can file a bankruptcy case – and additional counseling on budgeting and debt management before their debts can be wiped out. And, because the law imposes new requirements on lawyers, it is sometimes tougher to find an attorney to represent you in a bankruptcy case.

Here are some of the most important changes.

Restricted Eligibility for Chapter 7 Bankruptcy

Under the old rules, most filers could choose the type of bankruptcy that seemed best for them – and most chose Chapter 7 bankruptcy (liquidation) over Chapter 13 bankruptcy (repayment). The new law prohibits some filers with higher incomes from using Chapter 7 bankruptcy.

How High is Your Income?

Under the new rules, the first step in figuring out whether you can file for Chapter 7 bankruptcy is to measure your "current monthly income" against the median income for a household of your size in your state. If your income is less than or equal to the median, you can file for Chapter 7 bankruptcy. If it is more than the median, however, you must pass "the means test" – another requirement of the new law – in order to file for Chapter 7.

The Means Test

The purpose of the means test is to figure out whether you have enough disposable income, after subtracting certain allowed expenses and required debt payments, to make payments on a Chapter 13 plan. To find out whether you pass the means test, you subtract certain allowed expenses and debt payments from your current monthly income. If the income that's left over after these calculations is below a certain amount, you can file for Chapter 7.

(For more detailed information on these calculations and an online calculator that will do the math for you, see www.legalconsumer.com, created by Albin Renauer, co-author of Nolo's book *How to File for Chapter 7 Bankruptcy*.)

Counseling Requirements

Before you can file for bankruptcy under either Chapter 7 or Chapter 13, you must complete credit counseling with an agency approved by the United States Trustee's office. (To find an approved agency in your area, go to the Trustee's website, www.usdoj.gov/ust, and click "Credit Counseling and Debtor Education".) The purpose of this counseling is to give you an idea of whether you really need to file for bankruptcy or whether an informal repayment plan would get you back on your economic feet.

Counseling is required even if it's obvious that a repayment plan isn't feasible or you are facing debts that you find unfair and don't want to pay. You are required only to participate, not to go along with any repayment plan the agency proposes. However, if the agency does come up with a repayment plan, you will have to submit it to the court, along with a certificate showing that you completed the counseling, before you can file for bankruptcy.

Toward the end of your bankruptcy case, you'll have to attend another counseling session, this time to learn personal financial management. Only after you submit proof to the court that you fulfilled this requirement can you get a bankruptcy discharge wiping out your debts. (The website above also lists approved debt counselors.)

Lawyers May Be Harder to Find – and More Expensive

As you can see, the new law adds some complicated requirements to the field of bankruptcy. This makes it more expensive – and time-consuming – for lawyers to represent clients in bankruptcy cases, which means attorney fees, have gone up.

The new law also imposes some additional requirements on lawyers, chief among them that the lawyer must personally vouch for the accuracy of all of the information their clients provide them. This means attorneys have to spend more time on bankruptcy cases, and charge their clients accordingly. This combination of new requirements have driven some bankruptcy lawyers out of the field altogether.

Some Chapter 13 Filers Will Have to Live on Less

Under the old rules, people who filed under Chapter 13 had to devote all of their disposable income – what they had left after paying their actual living expenses – to their repayment plan. The new law added a wrinkle to this equation: Although Chapter 13 filers still have to hand over all of their disposable income, they have to calculate their disposable income using *allowed* expense amounts dictated by the IRS – not their actual expenses – if their income is higher than the median in their state. And these allowed expense amounts must be subtracted not from the filer's actual earnings each month, but from the filer's average income during the six months before filing.

Other Changes

There are other changes that can affect bankruptcy filers negatively, including how property is valued (at replacement cost instead of auction value) – this means more debtors are at risk of having their property taken and sold by the trustee – and how long a filer must live in a state to use that state's exemption laws (this can make a big difference in the amount of property a bankruptcy filer gets to hold on to). These changes and others are explained in *The New Bankruptcy: Will It Work for You?*, by Attorney Stephen Elias (Nolo).

❧ SUMMARY ❧

Like any major decision in life, the decision to file either of the options under the personal Bankruptcy code afforded us as consumers is a very personal decision. No one should influence your decision, including me.

I have tried to lay out as best I could the process and what I think are the positive and negative aspects of both forms of BK protection. So many factors went into our decision to file the Chapter 13, with the main reason being keeping the house. I have been told that this is the most common reason for most people to file the Chapter 13.

There is no doubt that the repayment plan we agreed to pay was stretching us so thin that it was almost not worth it. Looking back it certainly would have been much easier if we had just packed it in and moved to an apartment for a year or two and slowly gotten back on our feet again.

The greatest positive it accomplished was to help my wife and I see how resilient we could be. We went to work to get our financial lives in order and as of this writing we continue to be blessed. Since I already knew what hard work was, getting those second jobs to keep the payments to the trustee current got old in a hurry. We have worked hard to insure that this will never happen again and we pray that if it does we will have what it takes to get through it again.

For all of you who feel that filing for BK protection carries a negative stigma, forget about that. While attempting to help people in foreclosure and seeing the negative side of debt, I also have studied people who have accumulated great wealth.

You should know that many very successful people in America, before they came to be financially successful, went through a personal BK at one point in their lives. This fact was one that I held on to while we were going through ours. I knew that we could and would get out of the mess and come out financially stronger on the other side.

You can too, just keep your sights on what you want in life, combine it with a burning desire for it's achievement, and there is nothing that will keep it from becoming a reality. Never loose hope and never give up the fight.

In the next chapter we will get into ways and resources to improve your credit. I will discuss credit counseling and some real steps you can take to get back on your feet credit wise. We will also explore a few credit myths that will be exposed and busted. Let's move on to chapter nine.

Chapter 9

Your Credit – Credit Counselors, Credit Scoring Myths & How to Get Back On Your Feet Financially

⚜ CREDIT COUNSELING, THE GOOD, BAD, & THE UGLY ⚜

Like everything else in life, not all credit counselors are created or get results equally. There are as many good agencies out there as there are bad. We will discuss some of my ideas for the best route to take when working with a credit counselor, what rip offs to look for and how to protect you from people who take advantage of people with credit issues.

Today you can find the Consumer Credit Counseling Service in just about every city. A decade or so ago, the consumer credit counseling industry was dominated by the National Foundation for Credit Counseling, who's affiliates where non-profit, usually known as the Consumer Credit Counseling Service. They help to negotiate lower interest rates and assist to structure repayment plans for people who had fallen behind on payments.

As you have probably seen both on television and the Internet, these types of services have plenty of competition. The flood of consumer debt in the 1990's has aided in the creation of hundreds of competitors. Some of these companies have slick marketing with similar names and almost too good to be true come-ons via the Internet.

As mentioned above, some are better than others at renegotiating payment options. There fee structure varies from a big upfront fee to pay their high priced executives and end up pocketing much of the money that should be going to pay off your creditors. Some of these companies are just focusing their marketing on people who are just ticked off over their high interest rates and aren't even behind on their payment yet.

Be extremely careful when contacted by these "debt elimination companies" that promise that for a fee, usually in the thousands of dollars, they can eliminate all your debt. We are even seeing this in the mortgage arena where the claim is they can erase your mortgage completely. Although I have researched this myself, I am not convinced this is a legitimate way to get out of debt.

Even if by chance it were, I would have a very hard time morally getting away with the debt elimination knowing that I signed on the dotted line to repay the debt. I just try and do the right thing.

With Americans' carrying more personal debt than in any time in history, there are more and more of these companies sprouting up all the time. With this debt also comes a rise in personal bankruptcy fillings as we discussed earlier.

Some statistics dating back to 2001 estimated that 560,000 or so people enrolled the services of some kind of credit counselor. A closer look at the statistics further show that nearly half of the people working the credit counseling route fell out of the payment plan with some opting for the personal bankruptcy option.

The main task of the credit counselors is to negotiate lower payments with credit card companies and other lenders. They basically make the payment on your behalf from the funds you have sent the credit counseling agency via an electronic funds transfer or by check.

The fees collected by the counseling services are most times collected from the lenders themselves in a form of percentage payment for whatever is paid by their clients. There has been some question if this arrangement constitutes a conflict of interest for the credit counselors. Since they are collecting their fees from the credit card companies, some feel they are just a tool for the lending company. I report, you decide!

What has hurt the companies that are truly helping the consumer is the rise of new companies targeting customers who are just looking for those lower interest rates. These companies end up hurting the people they are supposed to be helping by negatively affecting their credit ratings while going through the process.

The sad fact is that you can negotiate lower interest rates on your own. Just call up your credit card company and ask. It would also help to mention to them that you are seriously looking at moving your account balance over to a new company with very low interest rates. A veiled threat never hurt anyone, just be prepared to back it up and move your account if you get no satisfaction. Just don't go paying someone to do something you can do on your own.

If you are too far in debt, credit counseling may not be able to help. There are limits to how little your creditors will accept, and a credit counseling service may not be able to cut your payments enough to either give you breathing room or get you out of debt. If that's true, bankruptcy may be the best of the bad options.

The following guidelines are what to consider when contemplating whether using the services of a credit counselor:

-Are you consistently late paying one or more of your regular bills?

-Are creditors and collection companies constantly hounding you?

-Are you failing to pay just the minimums due on your credit card payments?

-Have you tried to work out a reasonable repayment plan with your creditors and those efforts have failed?

Whatever payment plan is worked out, the plan should not call for your payments to stretch out for many years. The typical plan ranges from two to four years. If the credit counselor does not offer the option of a bankruptcy or payment plans longer than four years, they are not doing their job.

If you have made the decision to use the services of a credit counselor, the following section will highlight what to look for and what to beware of.

Be on the lookout for companies who charge big up front fees for their services. Most charge a set-up fee that should be under $25 in most all cases. If the set-up fees are much higher, ask specifically what you are getting for your money and don't sign anything until you know what you are paying for.

If you are going to deal with a credit-counseling agency, you should look for some sort of accreditation from a national association. The two prominent associations are the National Foundation for Credit Counseling and the Association of Independent Consumer Counseling Agencies.

Be sure that your payments are making their way to your creditors. There are some companies that will keep the first months payment as their fees for getting your repayment plan negotiated. Be careful, if this is their practice to collect their fees, it may adversely affect your credit. It is your right to ask for an accounting of what your monthly payment is paying. Get them to supply a breakdown of who was paid what amount for any particular month.

Use some common sense when it comes to the promises made by these companies. If it sounds too good to be true, it usually is. Their goal should be to assist you in getting your debt paid and minimizing the damage to your credit rating, nothing more, and nothing less.

It is true that in some cases that reverting to a credit counseling company may have a negative effect on your credit; however it is much easier to recover from late or slow payments on your credit report than a full blown bankruptcy.

I know first hand that no matter how we thought we were doing a good thing by filing the Chapter 13 and repaying everyone, the bankruptcy on our credit was the kiss of death for us. Most lenders would prefer to do business with customers with good credit; consequently they will typically not do business with you for the 10 years the bankruptcy remains on your file.

The truth is that the discretion of the future lenders who look over your credit report will determine your credit worthiness in the future. Some will look at credit counseling negatively, and other will not care. It really boils down to how your lenders will report your account to the various credit bureaus.

First USA, the credit card giant, reports its customers as delinquent on their bills until they make three consecutive payments of the new minimums negotiated by their credit services. Citibank, for contrast, simply adds a note to the credit bureaus' files that the customer is enrolled in credit counseling.

Being reported as late or delinquent can certainly hurt your credit score, the three-digit number widely used by lenders to determine your creditworthiness. A simple notation about your credit counseling probably won't. The credit score formula used by most lenders, known as FICO, now ignores any references to credit counseling that may be in your file.

Even some lenders that were traditionally suspicious of credit counseling have loosened their position. More mortgage lenders are willing to lend to people who have successfully completed repayment plans.

Some lenders even go as far as to say that they view credit counseling as an encouraging sign that a customer is getting his or her debts under control. Citibank, the largest issuer of credit cards, says people who have fallen behind on their payments often improve their status in the company's eyes by enrolling in and sticking with a debt repayment plan.

With that said, there are still some lenders who will refuse to deal with anyone who has enrolled in credit counseling. And if you fell behind on your payments before you entered credit counseling, you'll find those late payments will still affect your credit score even after you have paid off your debts.

There is much to consider when deciding to work with a credit counselor. Know your options and don't make a bad situation worse by getting into something you will regret later on.

⚜ CREDIT SCORING MYTHS ⚜

There is a tremendous amount of misinformation when it comes to what does and what does not affect your credit score. The sad fact is that most of this bogus information is coming straight from the mortgage lenders who should know better.

In my business, I work with quite a few excellent mortgage brokers and mortgage lenders who really know their business. They keep up with the latest trends in lending, know of all the new programs being offered and do their best to work with the clients we send them. They know what information is available to them when it comes to credit scoring. That's important, because the FICO credit score, in its various forms, is used in three-quarters of all mortgage lending.

If you do get out there and you are working with a mortgage broker or mortgage lender and they give you any of the following "tips," get up quickly and find another broker or lender.

❧ MYTH #1: CLOSING ACCOUNTS CAN HELP YOUR CREDIT SCORE ❧

Closing accounts can never help your credit score; on the contrary, it may hurt it. It is very true that having too many open accounts can hurt your score, but the damage was already done when you opened the account. Bottom line is that you can't repair it by shutting the account, and you may actually make things worse.

The credit score looks at the difference between your available credit and what you're using. If you shut down accounts, and your credit shrinks, this causes your outstanding balances to look even larger, which typically hurts your credit score.

The credit score also tracks the length of your credit history. Shutting down older accounts can also make your credit history look younger than it actually is. Lenders look for stability in payment histories, closing accounts can actually end up hurting your score.

Of course, credit scores aren't the only thing lenders look at when making credit decisions. They typically consider other factors such as your income, assets, employment history, and years in the same profession, and credit limits. Mortgage lenders in particular might look at your total available credit and ask you to close a few accounts as a condition for getting a new loan.

However, if your goal is to improve your credit score, you generally should not close accounts in advance of such a request. Best advice would be to pay down some of that credit card debt; this will actually work to improve your credit score.

❧ MYTH #2: CHECKING YOUR FICO (CREDIT) SCORE CAN HURT YOUR CREDIT. ❧

Generally speaking when you are applying for any new credit is what adversely affects your credit score. The fact is that ordering a copy of your own credit report does not count. Further, the mass inquiries made by credit card lenders who are trying to decide whether to send you an offer for a pre-approved card will not negatively hurt you either. That is, until you decide to take them up on their offer.

If you are looking to minimize the damage done from credit inquiries, make sure that when you shop for a mortgage you do so within a short time span. The FICO score treats multiple inquiries in a 14-day period as just one inquiry and ignores all inquiries made within 30 days prior to the day the score is computed.

The typical credit inquiry we are talking about that negatively affects your credit score usually results in no greater than a five-point drop in your score as a result. When we are talking of credit scores ranging from a low of 300 to a high of 850, the five points should not hurt you that badly.

❧ MYTH #3: CREDIT COUNSELING WILL HURT YOUR SCORE AS MUCH AS A BANKRUPTCY. ❧

The current FICO formula ignores any reference to credit counseling that may be in your file. That's been true for the last three years, after researchers at "Fair Isaac", the company that created the FICO scoring system, noticed that people getting credit counseling didn't default on their debts any more than anyone else who did not have credit counseling.

The mortgage lenders who don't like credit counseling generally treat its enrollees the same as if they had filled for Chapter 13 bankruptcy. The mortgage lenders look at people who have filled Chapter 13 more favorably than ones filling Chapter 7 for the simple fact that the Chapter 13 is a repayment plan and the Chapter 7 which allows you to erase most of your debt. You may still be able to qualify for a loan from one of these lenders, although your interest rates will almost certainly be higher than if you had perfect credit.

⚜ MYTH #4: YOUR FICO ISN'T THE ONLY SCORE YOU NEED TO CHECK. ⚜

This myth originated from lenders who erroneously thought the FICO score was offered by only one of the three major credit bureaus: Equifax.

In reality, all three of the bureaus offer FICO credit scores using the formula developed by Fair Isaac, but they each give the scores a different name. At Equifax, the FICO is known as the Beacon credit score. At TransUnion, it's called Empirica. At Experian, it goes by the strange title of "Experian/Fair Isaac Risk Model."

What complicates things for most people is that chances are you will have three different scores from each of the three credit reporting bureaus. This will occur primarily because the bureaus don't all share the same credit data. One bureau may list more accounts for you than another, for example, and the difference (in types of accounts, payment histories, credit limits and balances) will be reflected in the score that bureau computes for you.

Because of these potential differences, it does indeed make sense to pull and examine your credit reports from all three bureaus before you apply for a big loan like a home mortgage. Many mortgage lenders take the middle score from the three bureaus when making their decisions, so fixing errors in all three reports before you shop around for a loan is simply smart.

The bottom line is that the ways to improve your credit score is the same in all cases; correct all known errors on your report, pay your bills on time, pay down your debt, and apply for credit sparingly.

You can get copies of all three of your credit scores online at myFico. com.

❧ HOW TO PUMP UP YOUR CREDIT SCORE ❧

Some of the thoughts and strategies discussed in this section of the chapter may seem redundant; however I will get into a little greater detail as to why I am suggesting you do what I am telling you to do.

There are very few of us who have never in their lives had a problem with paying bills or making ends meet at one time in our lives or another. I am certainly no different. The fact is that you have plenty of company. There are more than 30 million people in the United States with credit blemishes severe enough (credit scores under 620) to make obtaining loans and credit cards with reasonable terms difficult.

There are also a slew of credit repair companies out there who will help you repair bruised and damaged credit. They charge a fee and like anything else out there do your homework and find out who has actually been successful in helping clients repair their damaged credit.

Even if your credit is good, it does not hurt to periodically have it pulled and check the data for accuracy. It will surprise you and maybe even tick you off at the amount of misinformation contained in your credit report. Remember humans impute the data into the credit bureau computers. Enough said.

What was once difficult information to obtain; the nuts and bolts information pertaining to what comprises a credit score is now readily accessible to everyone who wants it. The obvious place to start when trying to repair your credit is to get a copy of the report.

Look for any obvious errors. One that appeared on my credit report was an open account at a department store I never heard of and had never set foot in. I wrote to them and told them such and after about three months it was removed from the report.

❧ PAY YOUR BILLS ON TIME ❧

Believe it or not, your payment history is the single most important factor in determining your credit score, making up 35% of the total weight of the credit score. Since your recent history carries more weight than what happened five years ago, getting in the habit of making payments on time is a sure fire way to start rebuilding your credit rating.

On the flip side, delinquent payments can quickly devastate your credit score. Missing even one payment can knock 50 to 100 points off a good score. Skipping payments for a single month on all your bills can lower your credit score from a respectable 710 to a poor range of 560 to 630.

The tip I would pass along to people who need the discipline to get their bills paid on time is to use the many automatic payment plans the mortgage companies and utility companies offer their customers. You can give them access to your checking account for automatic withdrawals at a set date during the month. Paying bills online is also a great option that allows you to set up recurring payments with your online banking option. Although I have a personal bias against giving any company access to my checking account information, it may be just the discipline you need to get your bills paid on time.

❧ PAY CASH AND AVOID USING YOUR CHARGE CARDS / PAY DOWN DEBT ❧

The more debt you consistently pay down, the wider the gap between your balances and your credit limits. Lenders love to see plenty of breathing room between the amount of debt reported on your credit cards and your total credit limits.

What many people don't know is that credit scores don't distinguish between those who carry a balance on their cards and those who don't. So charging less can also improve your score, even if you pay off your credit card totals each month.

Your credit card issuer takes a look at your account about once a month and reports the outstanding balances on that day to the credit bureaus. This snapshot in time doesn't reflect whether you pay off that balance a few days later or whether you carry a balance from month to month.

If you do plan to apply for a mortgage, automobile loan or other major credit card account in the next year, start paying down those balances now. If you are in the habit of using plastic to pay for everything, as mentioned above, start paying with cash in the months before you do apply. This alone may help insure you get a lower interest rate for that next financed purchase.

❧ DON'T CLOSE OLD, PAID-OFF ACCOUNTS ❧

Although the temptation is great when rebuilding credit to pay off one old account in full and then close it so we never have to be reminded we ever had that account and carried the balance for so long. The fact is that closing paid off accounts can never help your score, and often it can end up hurting.

This knowledge is frustrating to those of us who want to simplify our lives and reduce the chances of identity theft by closing unused accounts. But we are playing on the credit company's back yard so don't fight the facts.

The facts is that shutting down credit accounts lowers the total credit available to you and makes any current outstanding balances you do have loom larger in credit score calculations. If you do close your oldest accounts, it can actually shorten the length of your reported credit history and make you seem less credit-worthy.

If you do carry outstanding balances or charge frequently, however, leave all your old accounts open, especially if you are about to apply for new credit. So next time you are in a major department store and they are offering you a 10% discount for signing up for a new card, remember that each new account can create a dent in your credit score. It also opens doors for credit thieves. Bottom line is that you should only apply for credit you really need.

❧ DON'T BE AFRAID OF CREDIT COUNSELING ❧

As mentioned earlier, the use of a qualified credit-counseling agency can help you to repair your damaged credit. By setting up a repayment plan, negotiating lower interest rates, and acting as a third party distributor of your payments, it can certainly get you back on track.

What used to be common practice by credit reporting bureaus has changed over the past few years. What used to be considered a stigma has now been replaced in many circles as a positive step by a consumer to get their financial act together. Furthermore, the references to credit counseling on your credit report are typically removed from a credit report after a consumer has successfully completed a repayment plan. That simply means there is no lasting reminder on your credit history.

As time goes on, fewer lenders still use the old scoring system that used to punish people working debt repayment plans. Others, particularly mortgage lenders, simply will not work with people in credit counseling until their plans are completed, regardless of their credit scores.

❧ STAY OUT OF BANKRUPTCY IF YOU CAN ❧

Ask me how I know this? Of all the mistakes we made, filing the bankruptcy was the biggest with respect to how hard it hurt our credit. Bankruptcy is the nuclear bomb of the credit world, worse than delinquencies, loans or collections. Its impact however, largely depends on how many black marks you had on you're credit before you filed.

Bankruptcy can knock 200 points or more off the score of someone with otherwise good credit. People with multiple delinquencies or collections on their report will see less of a decline because their scores are low to begin with. Either way, recovering from a bankruptcy can be tough. Once a score is pushed below 620, which bankruptcy inevitably does, credit becomes scarce and far more expensive.

High interest lenders love recent bankruptcies because they know consumers are not allowed to file Bankruptcy again for another six year. This gives them plenty of time to suck out many high interest rate payments. On the other hand, many mainstream lenders will generally reject consumers with a bankruptcy on their record. Bankruptcies are maintained on your credit report for up to 10 years.

Knowing your credit score and the potential impact of a bankruptcy might help you maintain your resolve and pay off your bills and improve your credit situation. Or, you make up your mind that since your credit is so trashed, it might not make matters much worse and file the bankruptcy anyway.

Finally on this subject, once you know the impact on your score a bankruptcy will cause, get good objective advise before taking the step to file bankruptcy. Most Attorneys may seem overly eager for you to file while credit counselors advise you that you should not. Remember their motivations and how they get paid and make a decision that is in your best interest.

It would also make sense to go back in the previous chapter and review all the new Bankruptcy law changes that are now law.

Now that you are on your way to repairing your credit, I will show you some ways to buy properties with no cash or credit. We now move on to Chapter 10 for a crash course in my world of real estate investing where we go against conventional wisdom and get what we want on our terms.

Chapter 10

Buying a House With Bad or NO Credit

❧ NOW THAT YOU SURVIVED FORECLOSURE, IT'S TIME TO RE-BUILD! ❧

The bad news is that if you just went through a full- blown foreclosure or if you have filed for bankruptcy, the good news is that there is still an opportunity to buy a house and live in a nice house in a nice neighborhood.

As an investor and entrepreneur, I am here to tell you that you don't need credit or a huge down payment to buy another house. I'm sorry to have to break this news to you, but the fact of the matter is that what they advertise on those late night infomercials is true about buying houses with nothing down. It happens every week in my world and with just a little information on where to look; it will work for you too. Granted, every market across America is different, but I have bought properties both in the Northeast and down south with the same methods. It is simply a matter of finding a Seller motivated enough to live by the terms you have offered. Part of my FREE e-course available at www.clydegoulet.com will detail how you too can do this as well.

Are most of those get-rich quick late night programs rip-offs? I would just say this; make sure the people you study with are actually buying houses, not just selling their theory about how to do it. To follow are some of my tried and tested methods for buying properties with very little down and really no credit check. It will require some work, but in life is there really anything worthwhile that you ever accomplished that did not require some work?

If you have come to the point where you have been forced to vacate your home because of the foreclosure, you will need to look for a place to live. Preferably, this new housing will be comparable to where you were living before. You will want a good house in a safe neighborhood with good schools if you have school-aged children.

You will also need to look for a place that is affordable and will not require you to compromise your lifestyle too much. Is such a place really out there for you after all this negative activity in your life regarding your housing situation?

The following three sub-sections will describe a step-by-step process for what to look for in a property and the ideal situations to look for to get you back on the road of homeownership without those nasty banks and mortgage companies charging you fees and points. If I had known these techniques 25 years ago, I would have retired a long time ago.

⚜ LEASE/OPTION OR RENT-TO-OWN: ⚜

I have purchased dozens of properties in the manner that I am about to describe. The Lease/Option or Rent to Own method of buying a property requires you to locate the type of property owner who wants rental income without the problems of being a landlord. If you doubt that there are property owners that have become sick of being landlords, this is one of the main reason why investment property owners get out of the rental property business. You ask how can this be so?

The Lease/Option (LO) requires in most cases for the tenant/buyer (that's you) to be responsible for all repairs and maintenance on the property, the same as you would as if you were the owner. You should note that if a major mechanical system where to fail, that expense should be paid by the property owner and/or it should be spelled out in the LO agreement who's responsibility it is.

My first question to anyone who is selling a house is if they would be interested in entering into a LO agreement. I describe the benefits to the owners such as continued lease income, no repair and maintenance, and a tenant/buyer with a property owners' mentality as opposed to a renters' mentality.

I handle objections from sellers by saying that since I would be responsible for all the repairs and maintenance, wouldn't that end up saving them money in the long run. The bottom line is that some will, some won't, so what, someone else is waiting to do the deal you want. Next!

Since the object of your desire is to get back into a property for the purposes of making it your home for a long time, you will be asking for the longest term possible on your L/O agreement with the property owners. Since everything is a negotiable point in a L/O agreement, ask for more than you ever hope to receive. Don't get crazy, but the only way to see if you can get anything in life is to simply ask.

In my mind, there are five (5) major points in a L/O agreement that must work for you and the sellers in order to make the deal work. These five will be listed in what I deem to be the order of their importance. Make sure you cover all these points in your negotiation; otherwise you will open yourself up for potential problems down the road. This is not complicated, so don't make it difficult or harder than it really is.

❧ TERM OF LEASE: ❧

You should always try and negotiate as long an L/O term on the lease as possible. The simple reason is that by what amounts to tying the property up via the L/O agreement, you in essence control the asset. You will have the ability to do one of two things at the end of the lease term; either purchases the house yourself at the price you have negotiated, or sell the option to another buyer. When you stretch out the terms of the lease you control whatever future appreciation may take place on the house. On the flip side, if property values drop, that is the risk you will need to determine if you want to live with or not.

I always ask for a one-year term with five one-year options to renew for one additional year making a total of six years that I could potentially control this asset. I always want the option to exercise the option when I want and the ability to participate in the appreciation as mentioned before. If the seller wants out much sooner than six years, then see if they will drop the price or take less monthly. Use this as a negotiating point and always ask for the longest term possible.

Just a word of caution; it is much better to have five one-year options than a five year deal with one option year. It builds into the agreement some negotiating periods when the seller may want out and you are not ready. It does require you to watch the calendar and formally renew every year, but it builds into the agreement some flexibility as well.

❧ RENT CREDIT: ❧

Always ask your seller if they have agreed to work a L/O agreement with you to credit a portion of what you pay to them every month in the form of a lease payment towards the purchase price. For instance, if you have agreed to pay $1,000 per month for the lease agreement, you ask the seller to credit $400 of that payment towards the purchase price you have both agreed to.

What this does is helps you build up a huge down payment on your house. Since you are going to have to pay to live somewhere, shouldn't a portion of your payment go towards benefiting you and helping you with your down payment? Think about the amount of money that could be credited towards the purchase price in just 2 years. ($400 X 24 months = $9,600) This is real money and it would go a long way in helping you get permanent financing on this house when the time you comes for you to do so.

Use this point in your negotiating as much as possible. This point goes hand-in-hand with the term of the L/O agreement you have worked out with the sellers. If you do take the L/O agreement out to the last year, your potential saved up credited down payment has risen to an impressive $28,800. (72 months @ $400 per month) In my example we are using some simple, but very real numbers.

I have used this technique of buying properties where we could not get the seller to give us a credit on the amount they had quoted for the monthly lease payment. I got creative and said to the seller if I paid him an extra $200 per month on top of what he was asking, would he then be willing to give me a $450 credit monthly. After some thought, they agreed. We passed all but $100 of the added monthly cost on to the Tenant/Buyers we installed in the house. We still controlled the property at our price with a good rent credit.

Buying a House With Bad or NO Credit

✄ DOWN PAYMENT: ✄

Many sellers will insist on as large a down payment or L/O deposit as possible. This may be a deal killer if you are really strapped for cash and have no means of generating the funds. Most sellers will require something and in many cases your L/O down payment/deposit will be non-refundable if you do not exercise your L/O at the end of the term of the lease.

I have no problem with the non-refundable part, the seller is taking the house off the market and allowing you to tie up the property, it is only fair for them to receive some consideration for that. If the seller insists on having a down payment, I will ask if they would be willing to take the down payment in monthly installments. If they agree to this, I know I can structure a deal with this seller. If they demand a big up-front chunk of cash and I am not ready to spend the money, I will pass on the deal.

For our example, if the seller insists on a $5,000 non-refundable deposit, but will accept the down payment in equal monthly installments, our monthly payment will bump up to $1,100 per month for the first four years of the agreement. (48 months @ an extra $100 per month) If the seller is looking to get the down payment in just two years, just adjust your monthly payment up another $100 to $1,200 per month. When you think about it, the monthly payment shouldn't matter since you are being forced into a savings plan that will be used for the purchase of the house.

Say the house we are talking about is worth $120,000 and we have entered into our agreement with the seller. After six years we will need to finance through a bank or mortgage company the amount of $86,400 calculated as follows:

Purchase Contract Price:	$120,000
Forced Down Payment (48 Months @ $100)	-$ 4,800
Monthly Credit (72 Months @ $400)	-$28,800
Amount to Finance:	$ 86,400

I am also going to assume the property appreciated a modest 2% a year for those five years making the current market value somewhere near $132,500. Your new loan with a loan to value ratio of 65% ($86,400 divided by $132,500) is very safe for any bank or mortgage company; regardless of you're past credit problems.

✖ PRICE: ✖

The price of the house we are looking for under a L/O agreement is not nearly as important as the terms that are part of the agreement above. It makes no difference to me if I pay full market price for a house if the terms are such that I will guarantee myself a big chunk of equity at the end of the lease term.

Many times you will find that sellers are blinded by price alone and will not budge from their vision of what their house is worth. The sellers were told that the Smith's house just three doors down sold for X amount and that since their house has brand new shower curtains it should sell for considerably more. The reasons for the price should be compelling and if you do have serious doubts, agree to have an appraisal done by an independent appraiser with the cost split 50/50.

If the price is within reason as to what the true market value is, then I have no problem. If it is way out of line and the seller will not move down to true market price, I will move on to a more reasonable seller and make the deal with someone else.

To me the L/O agreement affords me all sorts of latitude as an investor that a straight purchase will not. I can pay market price with the terms being such that I will be receiving a big monthly credit towards the purchase price as well as controlling an appreciating asset for as long as I have been able to negotiate the term of the deal.

When the time comes that I do want to place permanent financing on the property, I have a property that I will have no problems getting financing on since my loan to value ratio will be safe and attractive to lenders.

I should also add that the L/O agreement benefits the sellers as well. They no longer have to deal with the everyday bothers of rental property since you have agreed to handle all the repairs and maintenance on the property. And why shouldn't you, you are slowly acquiring more of an ownership interest every month. If your plans are to stay in the house for a long time, you are improving and maintaining the property that will soon be yours without the L/O agreement.

If you should default, the seller also has the ability to keep your non-refundable deposit as compensation for taking the property off the market. If you should fail to make your monthly payments, they have the right to evict you. In most states this process is much less time consuming and costly then foreclosing. Since we don't want to deal with that again, we will move on.

❧ MONTHLY PAYMENT: ❧

I know that some of you reading this will think that this should have been the most important piece of the puzzle. It may be for some, but think about the goal of getting back into your own house. I know that many people who have owned their own residence find it very difficult to be a renter again, living so close to neighbors that you can hear what is going on through the walls.

With that said, if you have worked out some great terms of the L/O agreement and you have found a seller to work with you, and the house is in the area you want to live, you are on the road to getting back on your feet. If you have structured your monthly payments with a healthy credit towards the down payment and you have a few years to pull off the final purchase, buckle down and work hard to make it happen.

I think I have the right to tell people what I am about to tell you because I have been there and done that. I am telling you that if you have been blessed with an opportunity such as this, don't blow it. If the payment is about $200 more per month than you can currently afford, then get out and get a second job that will pay you that extra $200 per month. Do whatever it takes to get through it and make it happen.

There was a time when I was in night school that I worked my full time nine to five job, went to school nights from 6:00 P.M. to 9:00 P.M. and then after classes, cleaned offices for some extra money. My wife and I were struggling to make ends meet, but we were working hard towards common goals. I can't stress enough how important it is not only to your basic housing needs but your financial future you make this work. This single strategy can get you back on your financial feet; please don't discount the importance.

◇◇ OWNER FINANCING FROM SELLERS: ◇◇

There was a statistic I read that was part of a real estate article where some research was done on the amount of property owners that owned their properties free and clear. In other words, the property owners had no mortgage to pay off; they owned the properties outright. The statistic quoted was between 30 and 35% of all property owned is owned free and clear of any debt.

This should encourage people who are looking to get back into a house without having to go crawling back to a bank. When asking about a house, always ask if the sellers would be willing to offer any sort of owner financing. It is a question I always ask when we are looking to invest in a property. I can guarantee that you will not be shot or will any physical harm come to you simply by asking. Unless you ask and highlight the benefits, then you will never know, will you?

Why would anyone want to act as the bank and finance a property for you? Well, if you have checked what certificates of deposits are paying, that answer is pretty obvious. With some accounts earning a pitiful 1½% to 3% in conventional savings accounts, don't you think that if a property owner is offered a rate of 7 to 9% on the equity in the property, they might just have to take a serious look at your proposal?

The other points in negotiating apply for this type of deal as well. As far as this or any other deal goes, the longer the term the better and the lower the down payment the better. There may be a balloon payment due in three to ten years, as most sellers do not want to wait the entire 30 years of a conventional loan to get all their money out. Again, price is not as important to me in deals such as this as long as the terms are favorable. I will always try for a lower price, but the bottom line is the control of the property is what I look for as an investor.

I always ask for 5% as the interest rate from any seller who may consider owner financing and move up. Think about it on the sellers end; they can put the equity in the property to work and create a steady monthly cash flow from the asset that was otherwise sitting idle. It serves a couple of purposes tax wise as well.

If they were to sell the property outright, they could be subject to a big tax bill from Uncle Sam because of the sale. If they sell it via owner financing, they are allowed to pay tax on only the amount of the gain realized in that particular year. This is called the installment sale and sellers should always seek competent advice from a tax professional.

For you the buyer, you are getting into a property where you have received financing from a source outside the bank. This means no points, junk fees, and other red tape associated with getting bank financing. You have all the rights of ownership and can sell the property at any time. On many occasions when we have obtained owner financing, the sellers never had a credit check generated on me. Not that I had anything to worry about, it is just an illustration that the process may be much more simple then you think.

Again, the bottom line is that the opportunity is such that you should try every means to make it work out financially. Make sure you have an attorney or competent title company check your documents to make sure you are all protected.

The owner financing is much easier than dealing with banks, but your responsibilities as a borrower are the same. The difference is that we are dealing with individuals and not big institutions. In my mind this makes our responsibility as the borrower even greater than if we were dealing with a bank. The seller has much more to lose and they do not have the luxury of passing on a bad loss to other borrowers down the line. Your relationship with the sellers financing the deal should be positive and professional.

Please do everything in your power to keep your end of the bargain. If something unforeseen should happen and you will not be able to pay the seller their money, think seriously about minimizing the time and money it will cost the sellers to get you out of the property. Do them a favor and vacate the property without having them spend more money to foreclose. It will be up to you, but consider whom you are dealing with.

❧ LAND CONTRACT / CONTRACT FOR DEED: ❧

Since every state has a different definition for how these two documents operate, the discussion will be in general terms and basically what they can do for you in the goal to owning your own home again. They are simply agreements that will enable you to control a property until you either take the sellers out or hand them back the property.

The Land Contract and Contract for Deed in their basic terms will be an agreement that will stipulate that you the buyer will make payments for a set period of time until certain conditions outlined in the agreement are met. You have all the rights of ownership and can sell the property or the rights to the property at any time, unless stipulated by provisions in the agreement that would forbid you to transfer rights.

In the handful of Contracts for Deed that I have been involved in, we were making payments to a property owner who did not want to enter a lease option agreement nor did they want to sell with owner financing since they had underlying financing that needed to be paid. Our agreement was that we would take over the property, including all repairs, maintenance, taxes, and insurance expenses for a period of at least 12 months.

The seller was requesting that we could not sell this property or refinance for at least one year due to some tax issues of the seller. He also had existing financing on the property that carried a pre-payment penalty for an early payoff. I simply agreed to make his payments directly to the mortgage company, pay him $150.00 per month and agreed not to sell or refinance for at least a year. After that year, I had done all I was supposed to do per the contract for deed and refinanced the property, got his mortgage paid off, kept in line with the sellers tax situation, and in the meantime the property appreciated almost 10%. This turned out to be a good deal for everyone involved.

For more in depth information on any number of buying techniques, you can always visit my website at www.clydegoulet.com

I ask you that you use all the information in this book as intended and for your best interest. With that said, there are techniques that I have been taught that could without a doubt be used to basically screw people out of their houses. Knowing what I do about the foreclosure process and how to control property for long periods of time, I will never be without shelter. On the flip side, I pray that I will never take advantage of the situation that a homeowner is in and make money off of their misfortune. There are enough so called investors who look for the greater fool and take advantage of situations I could not bring myself to exploit.

Be careful whom you deal with and make sure they are serving your best interest.

As we move to the last few chapters of this survival guide, please take the next few chapters for what is intended, my testimony to my faith and my belief that what has happened in my life has all led me here today to write this book in the hopes of helping someone realize that there are greater works left to be done. Excuse me as I climb aboard my soapbox and tell you of how God, the Supreme Being, Creator, whatever you call that Higher Power has changed my life and the benefits and rewards of giving. Hang on; the ride is almost over.

Chapter 11

Protect Yourself At All Times

There is an old saying that goes something like this: "If you don't look out for yourself, no one else will." There could be no truer words spoken when dealing with a foreclosure and all the activity that surrounds a foreclosure action.

Regardless of what may seem like good intentions from others, only you can decide what is best for you. As I mentioned earlier in this book, there are people who will try and separate you from whatever equity (cash) you may have in the property. Some will make no attempt to disguise what they are doing; others will try and be more cunning.

You need to know exactly what is in your best interest and the person you are dealing with should have the character and professionalism to tell you the truth, the whole truth, and nothing but the truth. And if you have a Bible handy, make them put their hand on while they are giving their pitch. O.K., maybe not that far!

This chapter was added because like everything in life, things change. This chapter is an update of current changes and will add to the already solid information contained in the previous 10 chapters.

The concept of doing in what is in your best interest is pretty much common sense and human nature. Not too many people are willing to knowingly hurt themselves if they are given all the options ahead of time and the consequences carefully explained. Here is some information that was omitted in the first 10 chapters.

They were not included because to be honest, it had not crossed my mind to include the information. The second reason was that things have and are always changing in this area of distressed properties. Here are a few added topics:

❧ ADDENDUM ON YOUR SHORT SALE CONTRACTS ❧

When I am submitting a contract asking the lender to accept a Short Sale payoff on behalf of a client I am representing, I always add an addendum. That addendum will read something like this:

1.   This contract is contingent on the mortgage holder (Insert Name of Bank/Mortgage Co.) agreeing to the "short sale" payoff detailed on the estimated HUD-1 enclosed and made part of the short sale package submitted by the broker/agent/ third party representative in the transaction.

2.   This offer is also contingent on the lender (Insert Name of Bank/Mortgage Co.) not seeking a deficiency judgment on the borrowers (insert name of borrowers).

If there happens to be a second mortgage on this property, then another addendum would be added that would state that the Short Sale is also contingent on both First and Second mortgage holders agreeing to the Short Sale.

The main reason I insert this wording on every contract I submit is that I want it made crystal clear right up front to the lender who is thinking about doing a Short Sale that they will not come after my client seeking a deficiency judgment. I have the lender make that call.

If the lender raises a stink and states that they will not do the deal with that wording in the contract, I then ask the seller to make the call. I will explain that a judgment may be awarded to the lender for any deficiency, but that does not mean that they will be able to collect.

If the seller I am representing decides they do not want to move forward, then the house will in all likelihood run the full course and be foreclosed. In most cases the lenders will grudgingly accept the wording and move forward with the Short Sale. Some lenders will not give it a second thought and still others will not even see that I have included it in the contract. I am not trying to "slip" anything by anyone, it is there in the contract and I even bring it to their attention.

The real downside of working a Short Sale on a property is the possibility of the lender being granted a deficiency judgment by the courts. The bottom line is though, if you have just disposed of your property and you had to use the Short Sale route to get that done, you have no money to pay them and the lenders know that.

What happens in many instances is that the judgment is sold to a debt collection company for pennies on the dollar and they then turn around and try and get their money back and then some. This judgment will certainly appear on your credit report and will have a negative impact. Will it have as big of an impact as a full blown foreclosure? With all the information I have researched and have been given, it will not.

Finally on this subject, you should know that all judgments have a shelf life. After so many years, and it varies from state to state, the judgment will just go away if it is not renewed through the courts. Let me give you two real life examples that I experienced and then we will move on.

Case # 1

I was just starting out investing in Florida and contracted with a seller selling their house on their own. I made the very dumb mistake of giving the Seller a $3,000 deposit on the house along with a contract. To make a long story shorter, they refused to close on the property and kept my $3,000. I got a judgment against them and they later sold the house to someone else, moved out of the state and I never recovered that money. That was a $3,000 real estate seminar that I took that did not involve sitting in a classroom.

Case # 2

A few years later I had a tenant in a property that stopped paying rent and after evicting them I obtained a judgment against them for back rent, legal fees and interest. After about 2 and ½ years I get a call from a mortgage broker working for these old tenants trying to get them a loan on a house they were trying to buy. They asked me if I would release the judgment. Well, I wasn't feeling very generous that day, so I told them that I would release the judgment when it was paid in full.

Five days later, I received the paperwork that would release the judgment along with a check for payment in full with a notary who had me sign off on the paperwork. I did agree to back off on the interest and they were able to purchase their house.

I just feel it is in your best interest to address the issue of the potential deficiency judgment up front and right away. I want there to be no question in anyone's mind where all parties stand before the deal will be approved. I don't want my clients being surprised by something that may kill the deal and keep me from earning a commission as a real estate broker. I also don't want my client being hit with this judgment when they don't have to.

FORGIVEN DEBT TREATED AS INCOME

At the end of Chapter three was a copy of the recent bill passed in Congress that addresses this provision, until the end of 2009 that is. To follow is what the potential pitfalls will be once that law expires and the Internal Revenue code reverts back to where forgiven debt is once again treated as income. As always, I will strongly suggest you consult a good Tax Attorney or CPA who stays up on all of the latest IRS ruling and changes in Tax policy.

Our very good friends at the Internal Revenue Service (IRS) have a provision in the tax code that states that any debt that is forgiven can be treated as "income" by the person who has had the debt forgiven. Now what does that mean to you as a borrower?

It means that if the lender so chooses, they can issue you a 1099 that would state that the amount they may have taken as a discount in order to sell your property via a Short Sale is income to you in the eyes of the IRS. Since I am not a CPA or an attorney, all I can tell you is to get competent legal advice on this issue.

Although many lenders have the right to issue you a 1099, many will not have the personnel within their companies to keep track of this bookkeeping process. Now the IRS states that we are to report all our "income" on our own and claim this "income" on our tax returns. Whatever happened to our rights to not incriminate ourselves?

So, if I understand this clearly, the lenders will get the benefit on the corporate side to write off this bad debt against their potential corporate earnings. Did the lender really get hurt or have a financial loss at all?

On the consumer side, the borrower who lost his house and maybe some equity (cash) as well might have to claim some debt that was written off by the lender as "income" and be subject to tax on money he never actually had in his hand. I guess in the world of the IRS this makes sense. And they wonder why more and more people every year are just flat out not filing returns.

Only you can decide how you would like to handle this potential situation. I have talked to a couple of CPAs' who told me that if a tax payer is declared "insolvent" in the eyes of the IRS, then they would not be required to pay the tax that might be due on this "income."

But that in itself is a problem. When you have to rely on the IRS to do the right thing, you are in trouble. As of this time, there is talk of legislation being proposed to address this issue on a permanent basis. I do hope they do the right thing for the people who may be staring at this. There is no reason to further burden someone who has lost their property or was forced to sell their property with this additional financial hardship.

The bottom line is to ask someone who understands this issue better than I do. It is something you need to be aware of and plan for just in case.

LOAN MODIFICATIONS

In an earlier edition of this book I stated that lenders very rarely got into doing Loan Modifications (LM) for borrowers. Well, with the recent flood of foreclosures, this is changing also. Many more lenders are seeing the LM process as a means for keeping good customers who have been paying on time with their soon-to-be adjustable rate mortgages ready to go up.

It is a smart, actually a very smart idea by these lenders to try and rewrite these mortgages via LM agreements that keep the already current payments at the same level. Many lenders are converting these Adjustable Rate Mortgages (ARM) to fixed rates in an effort to stem the tide of the foreclosure tsunami sweeping this country.

The further good news is that many lenders are also looking at the LM option even if the property owner has fallen behind. If you keep this fact in the back of your mind: Banks and mortgage companies are not in the business of owning real estate, then you will always know where they really stand, no matter what type of fertilizer you may be getting from the lender.

As I mentioned earlier, the LM may be as simple as converting an ARM to a fixed rate. Or it could be as complicated as taking the amounts of payments that may be in arrears and adding it to the principal balance and extending the years left on the loan. In the world of the LM, everything is negotiable.

With everything positive, there always seems to be the potential negative. If your loan is being handled by a Loan Servicing company, their hands may be tied. Let me explain what a Loan Servicing company does.

Some of the major loan servicing companies now operating is:

OCWEN (When spelled backwards is "New Co.")
ASC (America's Servicing Company)
Litton Loan Servicing
AMC Mortgage Servicing

The best way to explain how these companies operate is that they are like a Property Management Company for loans. They contract with the company or agency that owns the Mortgage Note to collect the monthly payment, make sure insurance is on the property, and both the real estate taxes and insurance premiums are paid from the accounts escrow account.

For this service, they are paid a fee, very similar to a management fee paid to a property management company.

When the property is in the foreclosure process, these servicing companies may be on the front lines acting as the Loss Mitigator's, but the ultimate decision is always made by the company or agency that owns the mortgage instrument. Does this make sense?

It took me a while to figure this out, but as I worked with more and more of these companies it dawned on me that the deals where the communication and speed of responses was the worst, were the deals where Loan Servicing Companies were involved. It made sense, they were not the ultimate decision makers and therefore all communication took longer.

Think of it for a minute. The person you are dealing with at the servicing company must get whatever you submit approved first by their supervisor and then and only then is it sent to the person handling that mortgage in a company or agency outside of the servicing company. That person may need to get additional people to sign off on the Loan Modification as well.

You should just know that the LM is now a more viable option then ever before. If you are just alert as to who you are dealing with and that they would much rather have someone paying on a loan then having the property back, you are negotiating in a position of strength. This is a great opportunity for people to actually keep their homes and the lenders are now working with borrowers to make it happen.

It's about time!

❧ THE SUB-PRIME BAILOUT PLAN ❧

There has been so much information and misinformation about this subject that I have done a bit of research and found some articles that explain what all this is about.

It is always the case when the crap hits the fan like it has with this sub-prime mess that fingers start to be pointed at who is to "blame." Well, let me tell you there is plenty of "blame" to go around.

The consumers should take some of the blame, it was their decision to sign on the dotted line and extend their credit. The banks and lenders who lent the money should share some of the blame for allowing people to borrow money who had no business borrowing a dime. The sub-prime mortgage brokers who got many people to bite on those very low teaser rates and did not fully explain what would happen when the rates started to bump up also deserve some of the blame.

There should also be some mention that the major builders who have a vested interest in seeing the housing industry continue to boom had a say in this mess too. Investors who bought on speculation that the market would continue to be hot and that property values would continue to increase are also in the same hot water.

So, when it is all boiled down to its most simple explanation, what and who will the "bailout" plan help and who will it not help? Here is an explanation I found on the WEB:

"First off, this Sub-prime rate freeze plan does NOT affect all Sub-prime borrowers about to be dealt with higher resetting mortgage payments. That is the most important thing you need to know. It is not a fix-it-all plan and it will not stop foreclosures and defaults from rising in 2008!"

Sure, it may help a little, but the most I get out of this is a stab at restoring confidence into the credit markets that the government will be there to help if things get hairy.

Here is who the plan will work for:

a) ONLY loans made at the start of 2005 through July 30th, 2007

b) ONLY loans that will reset to higher rate between Jan 1st, 2008 through July 31, 2010

c) ONLY owner occupied borrowers (primary residence borrowers)

d) ONLY those borrowers who CAN afford 'teaser' payments & CAN'T afford resetting payments

e) ONLY those borrowers who CAN PROVE they cannot afford resetting payments

f) ONLY those borrowers who are making payments ON-TIME

So, this bailout completely eliminates speculative borrowers who used these teaser mortgage products to keep costs ultra low while they flipped their properties! It also eliminates any borrower who:

1) already had their teaser rate reset to a higher rate

2) already are missing payments

3) was savvy enough to avoid a teaser mortgage product but now pays a higher 30YR fixed rate"

You can find the full article at www.Urbandigs.com

There is nothing that will further in helping your situation then getting and absorbing all the information you can about the subject matter.

Only you know what is best for your situation and you should make your decisions based on what is best for you in both the short term and long term. Allow no one to force you or coerce you into making a decision that will not be in your best interest. The only way to know what is in your best interest is to have all the facts.

My hope is that this updated section will add to the information contained in the first 10 chapters. I would not have gone through the effort and time to add this information if I did not think it would be helpful or relevant.

My door is always open and my contact information is the same. If you would like to contact me with a specific question that was not covered in this book, please do not hesitate to call my office and leave me a time when it would be best to call you back. You could also e-mail me a question at crgcrest@msn.com but please allow for a few days for a response.

I wish you all the best, take care and may God bless.

Clyde R. Goulet
Entrepreneur Publishing, Inc.

If you are looking for more information, I offer a free e-course available at www.clydegoulet.com

We never sell or abuse confidential e-mail addresses and you can opt out at any time.

Chapter 12

You Get More From Life By Giving More

My wife and I have come a very long way in the last ten to thirteen years financially. I can trace it back to one single decision we made and it may surprise you when I tell you. The decision was that no matter how tight things were with the finances; we were going to start tithing our income.

For those of you not familiar with the term: it represents a donation of 10% of your net to charity or someone less fortunate than yourself. I would be lying if I told you we started right off at 10%, but we did build up to that figure after about four months and have not stopped since.

Basically, we made a decision back in 1995 when we were in the beginning stages of our bankruptcy that we were going to give away to charity 10% of whatever we earned no ifs, ands, or buts.

We were strapped beyond belief some months and had to borrow some money just once over a five-year period to make our payment to the trustee from the bankruptcy. The funny and almost miraculous part was that just when it seemed some times that we were going to be unable to make the payment, a commission would come in and we would have the money.

Before I go any further with my story and my thoughts on this subject, I by no means will tell you to forego feeding your children or taking care of your most basic of needs. I will tell you that the more you give, the more you get. It is a fact in my life and many people who I speak to on this subject have had the same results.

There seems to be a very real force in nature that will pay you back much more than you pay out. In my Christian faith, it is a leap of faith to believe that God will provide for me no matter what may happen in my life. I am a living testament to the powers of giving. For whatever reason, the people I know who have the most opportunities come their way also are the most generous as well.

There were many things that I learned during our severe financial difficulties and one of the major things that stood out was that no matter how much money I did or did not have, the money was not the thing that would determine if I was happy with life or not. My health and the relationship I have with my wife is something that does not carry a dollar figure.

The other thing that struck me was that how ill prepared I was to handle the stress, misinformation and the psychological aspects of a foreclosure and bankruptcy. I thought back then how beneficial it would have been to be able to read a book or talk to someone who had been through what I was going through and be able to just answer some basic questions.

My goal with this book was to help in some way and to maybe give hope that if we survived and later prospered, then maybe others could too. There is a passage from the book of Philippians in the Bible that I keep on my wall from chapter 3 verse 13 that states: "Forgetting what is behind...I press on toward the goal."

✖ GETTING MY PRIORITIES STRAIGHT: ✖

I know for sure that the foreclosure and bankruptcy slapped me upside the head and forced me to take a look at our priorities. Although our debt was not a direct result of charging so much frivolous stuff on our credit cards that we did not need, part of our financial problems was still routed in using credit unwisely. Being in debt to credit card companies is a loosing game. If all you can afford is the minimum payments, you will usually take about 35 years to pay off credit card debt of $10,000 or more.

Besides our decision to give more, we decided that we would limit the use credit cards for things we could save for instead, basically delaying gratification of all kinds. We did make an exception and that was that if any emergency car repairs we needed, and we could not pay from the checkbook, we could charge. Since we were able to keep a couple of credit cards out of the bankruptcy filing, we had to be careful with those cards and quickly decided to pay them off as fast as we could.

We also made the decision to run the car we had until the wheels fell off. We ended up giving that car away to a single mother with no transportation after we had put over 223,000 miles on it. Since it still ran pretty well even though it burned a little oil, we were happy to give it away to someone who really needed it. It was a great feeling when we signed over the title to the car and both my wife and I received the biggest hugs. It really is better to give than to receive.

The bottom line is that we made a decision to get our financial house in order and think twice before spending money. We also took more time in determining what a real "need" was as opposed to a "want". The important fact was as long as we had our house payment made, food in the fridge, and a little money set aside for emergencies, we had enough money for the time being. I would worry about creating real wealth later on.

The other major priority was our health. It is an old cliché, but it is still very true that without your health, nothing else really matters. We knew first hand what poor health could and would do if not taken care of. It is one of the things I pray for daily, good health.

As it turns out that my wife had another health challenge in the summer and fall of 2006. Mary was diagnosed with breast cancer. Her surgery was successful and as of her last six month check up in the Spring/Summer of 2008, she is still cancer free and enjoying life again.

And I have started to get very serious about dropping some excess weight that has been a constant companion for about 20 years. I used to joke with the doctor and tell him my weight was perfect, I just wasn't tall enough. According to his charts I would have had to be about 7 feet 10 inches tall to justify my weight.

I also came to the very grim reality at age 53 that you don't ever see any five foot eleven inch 295 pound ninety year old guys walking around. So the choice was simple, but the work to get the weight off is not. Although down a full 35 pounds, I still have a long way to go to get to my goal of 180 pounds. Wish me luck, I need it. Without our health, there really isn't much else that matters.

❧ WE ARE NOT OUR MISTAKES: ❧

Indulge me as I relay to you some of the very real lessons I learned while trying to get over some of the negative feelings that were going through my mind during and after our foreclosure and bankruptcy. As I mentioned, I did and continue to do much reading on the subject of the human psyche. Since I was so down on myself for letting these financial problems happen, I automatically felt that I was the mistake. Fact was, I made some mistakes, but I was not the mistake.

The book that taught me to get my mind set in the right direction was "Psycho-Cybernetics" by Maxwell Maltz. Dr. Maltz was a plastic surgeon by trade but found that many of his patients, even after undergoing plastic surgery could not erase or change their negative self-images. This book examines how our mind works and how to eliminate some if not all of the emotional scars we have, either scars from family members when we were growing up or self-inflicted scars. This book will help you realize that you are what you believe you are in your own mind.

If you think you are a failure and a screw-up, you will not disappoint yourself and act like a failure and a screw-up. If you view yourself as a human being who is basically competent and successful, you will act competent and successful. It is worth reading, as a matter of fact, I make it a point to read it every year, either at the end of December or beginning of January. It certainly helps set my mind in the right direction.

Since I had gotten my head straight about how we developed our financial problems, it was time to tackle the money part of the equation. The best book I read and again read once a year is "Think and Grow Rich" by Napoleon Hill. This book is a classic and you will see many similarities with this book and Psycho-Cybernetics when it pertains to working on your thinking. The basic premise is that we are what we think about on a daily basis. If you want your life to change, you must change what you think about on a daily basis.

Hill states, "whatever a human mind can conceive and believe; he can achieve". He talks about setting clear mental pictures of what you want in life and developing a burning desire for that thing. I challenge you to think of something in your life that you wanted with a passion. You thought about it all the time, it was an obsession in your thoughts and it was the first thing on your mind when you got up in the morning and the last thing you thought about before falling asleep.

I know that you have all wanted something so badly it was the only thing you thought about. I didn't realize how powerful this theory was until I was much older in life.

One story that relates to this is my desire to get a college degree. Out of five brothers, just one of my older brothers and I ever earned a degree from college. Growing up in very much a blue collar environment, for some reason education was never given the same importance as a full time job. I bought into that idea for a while, but after spending a year stocking shelves at a local grocery store after graduating from High School, I knew I had to go back to school.

I wont bore you with all the details, but after two years of junior college, I was working a full time job, taking night school classes and working a small part time job after night school classes cleaning offices. It took me about four and a half years to complete my degree requirements, but I wanted that degree so badly, nothing was going to stand in my way.

The main reason for relaying this story of my academic success is to impress upon you what a burning desire will do for you when you make a goal in your life as big as you can. The "Think and Grow Rich" principles can be translated into anything you have a burning desire for in your life. It is truly sad that there are millions of people who plod through life never seeing or utilizing their true potential, please don't be one of them.

Another book worth reading is one by Brian Tracy entitled: "Goals, How to Get Everything You Want – Faster Than You Ever Thought Possible".

This book will take you through the dynamics of how to set goals for all different aspects of your life.

From your financial, to your spiritual and community goals can be worked on with this great book. This book will help you unleash the awesome power that goal setting has on your subconscious mind and how your subconscious mind works on your goals while you are least expecting it to. This is another book that is worth re-reading from time to time when you begin to wander and loose focus on your target goals.

For example, one exercise Mr. Tracy suggests is to write your main goals everyday on a sheet of paper. The first time I did this exercise it amazed me that the goals that were of most importance to me were the ones I thought of constantly. It is no coincidence that these goals were reached well before my deadline. There is a power in goal setting that must not be overlooked. You owe it to yourself to set some goals, make them a burning desire and watch out.

As Mr. Tracy states in the book, "you are 10 times smarter, 10 times more capable, 10 times better than you think you are". Setting goals will unleash the creative, goal striving person we all are. Get this book and use it, you will be amazed. Just so you know, I have no stock in any of these publishers and will receive no financial gain whether you read them or not. They are simply the books and theories that have assisted me in getting back on my feet and much more focused on my goals.

NEVER STOP LEARNING:

Whatever you decide to take from this book or any other material you may have picked up to help you through your financial problems, please remember to never stop learning about what effects your life. For many people this book will be educational, for others it will be a reference book of sorts.

By reading this far you have set yourself apart from the people in life that are just along for the ride. I am constantly attending seminars and training sessions to learn more about real estate and marketing, my two great passions. You must never stop learning.

The person, who thinks they know it all, acts like a know-it-all. I can tell you this; I don't want a doctor or dentist working on me who last learned what he or she learned 20 years ago. Do you think that medicine and dentistry has changed some in the last 20 years? The doctors and dentists are constantly being <u>required</u> to take continuing education courses that bring them up to date with the latest changes in medicine and dentistry.

Would you want your CPA or accountant filling out your tax returns based on the IRS rules from 15 years ago or would you like him or her to have all the latest up to date information and changes to the IRS tax code?

You should always be striving to learn more, know more, and keep your mind searching for new and better opportunities, especially in the area of creating additional income. As mentioned in other areas of this book, I offer a free e-mail course on the Foreclosure process and how to get back on your financial feet. You can enroll in this free e-course at the www.clydegoulet.com web site.

Again, the best way to get what you want out of life is to give something back.

FINAL THOUGHTS:

Since I mentioned this topic briefly in chapter one, I will get back on my soapbox and hit you again. Please do not let your temporary financial setbacks define and scar you for life. The foreclosure process happens to hundreds of thousands of people every year, more so these past few years than ever before in our country's history. The bankruptcy process happens to hundreds of thousands every year. It is merely a bump in the road. Get over it and move on.

It is so easy to point fingers and try to lay blame on one or the other spouse. I have found that through my work with property owners that there is always one person out of the husband and wife team who handles the bulk of the household finance chores. There may be a degree of guilt such as I felt for allowing my financial mess to happen. Just don't get to that point in your thinking.

You must start focusing on the ties that bind you and your family together, not the points that separate. To be in a committed relationship there must have been a time of intense feelings for one another, you should not let pieces of paper with pictures of dead presidents tear those feelings apart. It is only money; it can be replaced. People and loved ones cannot.

If you have children, you must bring them into your thinking as well. You must pull together and work to help make a better life for them. Remember, they had no choice in being where they are; you have a responsibility to provide the best you can give. How you handle the temporary financial bump will be instructive to them as well. If you hadn't noticed, kids see everything and are 100 times more perceptive than we think they are.

If you do practice your faith, become more involved with the church or place of worship of your choice. In the depths of our financial problems, I was asked by a member of my church to help him out and volunteer one night at the agency that served hot meals to homeless people in our county. Talk about a wake up call out of the self-pity I was going through. We have more blessings in our lives than we can ever count.

I strongly suggest joining a faith based organization and giving something back that way. I was born a Catholic but currently attend an Episcopal church. My Aunt Teresa who is a Catholic nun and my mom's sister when I asked her about me attending an Episcopal church told me once. Her thoughts were that God would hear your prayers no matter where you are. She was right; there has never been a time when my prayers have not been answered. It may not have been on my timeline, but they were answered and they were answered at just the right time.

At this time my prayer for you is that your financial problems will soon be over, that your family and friends stay in tact, and that your future is bountiful in good health, good fortune, and Gods blessings.

About the Author

Clyde R. Goulet is considered by many experts one of the nations leading authorities on the Foreclosure process. Having first person experience in both the Foreclosure and Bankruptcy process, Clyde is uniquely qualified to speak and write on the subject. His "in the trenches" experience as a counselor to many property owners facing foreclosure or hard financial times extends to his personal business as a licensed real estate broker in central Florida.

Clyde grew up in the Northeast in the border town of Methuen Massachusetts. He has lived in Central Florida for over 18 years and is still very active in assisting property owners out of very tough financial times. He welcomes questions and comments via his e-mail address at crgcrest@msn.com or via his business phone at 407-688-2747.

Clyde has also taken up the charge to educate as many Realtors and real estate professionals as possible to assist property owners in the process of negotiating with the banks and mortgage companies to get their debt reduced. Having authored numerous articles on the subject of Short Sales (The negotiating of debt in order for a property owner to sell their homes when they owe more than the property is worth on the open market.) both online and in print publications, Clyde penned a no nonsense manual that has been the cornerstone and cause for so many Realtors staying in the game and making a living in the tough market of 2008. Anyone wanting to learn the nuts and bolts, A to Z process of how a Short Sale works is advised to download this landmark manual. It is still available online at www.nobsshortsales.com

Clyde has also done his best to educate property owners who wish to sell their properties on their own as well. Being an active Real Estate Broker, Clyde has been selling both his own investment properties and properties of clients for many years. Clyde developed a home study course that will literally save any property owner thousands of dollars in commissions. Clyde admittedly has sold more copies of this manual to Realtors, but offers the course to the general public as well. This manual can be seen at www.getyourfsbosold.com

For property owners needing more information or wanting to sign up for Clyde's FREE e-course, you can visit www.clydegoulet.com and click on the "FREE E-Course" link.

Other projects that Clyde has devoted time to include his newest book soon to be released entitled: "The Survival Guide To Investing In Florida." Anyone who may have an interest in Florida investing is invited to sign up for two free months of a cutting edge newsletter that Clyde will be personally involved with called: " The Florida Real Estate Investment Advisory." You are invited to visit www.flareinvestmentadvisory.com and sign up for the free two months.

1962822